Betty Crocker

ANNUAL RECIPES

2·0·0·9

DINNER MADE EASY

Betty Crocker

ANNUAL RECIPES

2·0·0·9

DINNER
MADE EASY

RODALE

Notice

Mention of specific companies, organizations, or authorities in this book does not imply
endorsement by the author or publisher, nor does mention of specific companies, organizations,
or authorities imply that they endorse this book, its author, or the publisher.

Internet addresses and telephone numbers given in this book
were accurate at the time it went to press.

Printed in the United States of America

Rodale Inc. makes every effort to use acid-free ∞, recycled paper ♻.

Book design by Christina Gaugler

ISBN-13 978–1–60529–883–2

ISBN-10 1–60529–883–2

2 4 6 8 10 9 7 5 3 1 hardcover

We inspire and enable people to improve their lives and the world around them
For more of our products visit **rodalestore.com** or call 800-848-4735

CONTENTS

INTRODUCTION

Dear Friends,

The phrase *supper's ready* means more than merely putting food on the table. It evokes the bond that families build when they break bread together. It's a respite from hectic modern life and an opportunity to reconnect with those we love.

Yet, for too many of us, cooking daily dinners has become a struggle. Lack of time for planning, shopping for special ingredients and doing the actual cooking is eroding this cherished time. However, there is a better alternative to carryout and convenience foods.

In this book, you'll find everything you need to create more than 215 easy and appealing suppers—more than 240 recipes in all—for every weeknight of the year. Think of it as your personal meal planner.

The unique format gives you an entire supper at a glance. Many are one-dish meals complete in themselves. Others include a main dish recipe and/or easy accompaniments for each meal. That means no more fumbling through pages and multiple chapters searching for several recipes to pull together a meal when everyone is hungry, tired and wants to eat NOW. Just open the book to the selected supper, and everything you need is right in front of you.

These are tried-and-true dishes that the family will love, made from ingredients that are pantry, refrigerator and freezer staples. If the fixings are at hand, meals come together fast.

With evening meals this simple, you can get down to the pleasure of sharing table time with family or friends.

Betty Crocker

CHAPTER 1

Satisfying Pasta, Pizza and Grain Suppers

Stuffed Pasta Shells

5 SERVINGS PREP TIME: **30 MINUTES** START TO FINISH: **55 MINUTES**

15 uncooked jumbo pasta shells

½ pound lean ground turkey

1 teaspoon Italian seasoning

½ teaspoon fennel seed

¼ teaspoon pepper

2 cups sliced mushrooms

1 medium onion, chopped (½ cup)

4 cloves garlic, finely chopped

1 cup fat-free cottage cheese

1 egg or 2 egg whites

2 cups tomato pasta sauce (any variety)

¼ cup shredded Parmesan cheese

1. Heat oven to 350°. Cook and drain pasta as directed on package, omitting salt.

2. While pasta is cooking, cook turkey, Italian seasoning, fennel seed and pepper in 10-inch nonstick skillet over medium heat 8 to 10 minutes, stirring occasionally, until turkey is no longer pink. Remove turkey mixture from skillet.

3. Cook mushrooms, onion and garlic in same skillet over medium heat 6 to 8 minutes, stirring occasionally, until vegetables are tender. Stir in turkey mixture, cottage cheese and egg.

4. Spray rectangular baking dish, 13 × 9 × 2 inches, with cooking spray. Spoon about 1 tablespoon turkey mixture into each pasta shell. Place in baking dish. Spoon pasta sauce over shells.

5. Cover with aluminum foil. Bake 20 to 25 minutes or until hot. Sprinkle with Parmesan cheese.

1 serving: Calories 370 (Calories from Fat 90); Fat 10g (Saturated 3g); Cholesterol 80mg; Sodium 810mg; Carbohydrate 44g (Dietary Fiber 4g); Protein 26g

MAKE IT A MEAL

Steam broccoli flowerets and drizzle with balsamic vinegar for a quick side veggie.

Tuscan Rigatoni with White Beans

6 SERVINGS PREP TIME: **10 MINUTES** START TO FINISH: **25 MINUTES**

2 cups uncooked rigatoni pasta (6 ounces)

1 large onion, chopped (1 cup)

1 package (1 pound) smoked turkey sausage, cut into ½-inch slices

1 can (15 to 16 ounces) cannellini beans, rinsed and drained

⅓ cup sun-dried tomatoes in oil, drained and chopped

⅓ cup chicken broth

1 tablespoon chopped fresh or 1 teaspoon dried rosemary leaves

⅓ cup shredded Parmesan cheese

1. Cook and drain pasta as directed on package.

2. While pasta is cooking, cook onion and sausage in 12-inch skillet over medium-high heat 2 to 3 minutes, stirring occasionally, until onion is tender.

3. Gently stir in pasta and remaining ingredients except cheese. Cook 3 to 5 minutes or until hot. Sprinkle each serving with cheese.

1 serving: Calories 400 (Calories from Fat 90); Fat 10g (Saturated 3g); Cholesterol 45mg; Sodium 970mg; Carbohydrate 55g (Dietary Fiber 5g); Protein 27g

MAKE IT A MEAL

Tuscany is a region in Italy noted for its white bean dishes and hearty breads. So round out this Tuscan skillet meal with a robust loaf of bread.

Fiery Fettuccine

4 SERVINGS PREP TIME: **10 MINUTES** START TO FINISH: **20 MINUTES**

8 ounces uncooked fettuccine

1 cup whipping (heavy) cream

1 teaspoon Cajun or Creole seasoning

1 jar (7 ounces) roasted red bell peppers, drained

½ pound fully cooked smoked sausage, cut into ¼-inch slices

2 medium green onions, sliced (2 tablespoons)

SPEED SUPPER
Substitute 1 container (7 ounces) refrigerated Roasted Pepper Cream Sauce for the whipping cream, Creole seasoning and roasted red bell peppers.

1. Cook and drain pasta as directed on package.

2. While pasta is cooking, place whipping cream, Cajun seasoning and bell peppers in blender or food processor. Cover and blend on high speed until smooth.

3. Pour pepper mixture into 12-inch skillet. Cook over medium heat, stirring occasionally, until mixture thickens. Stir in sausage and heat through but do not boil.

4. Serve sausage mixture over fettuccine. Sprinkle with onions.

1 serving: Calories 555 (Calories from Fat 335); Fat 37g (Saturated 18g); Cholesterol 145mg; Sodium 850 mg; Carbohydrate 43g (Dietary Fiber 2g); Protein 15g

MAKE IT A MEAL
Prepare your favorite spinach salad with this spirited pasta.

Chicken and Pasta Stir-Fry

4 SERVINGS PREP TIME: **10 MINUTES** START TO FINISH: **24 MINUTES**

2 cups uncooked farfalle (bow-tie) pasta (4 ounces)

1 pound asparagus, cut into 2-inch pieces (3 cups)

2 medium onions, sliced

1½ cups chicken broth

1 pound boneless, skinless chicken breasts, cut into 1-inch pieces

3 tablespoons chopped fresh or 1 tablespoon dried basil leaves

3 tablespoons chopped sun-dried tomatoes (not in oil)

¼ teaspoon pepper

Grated Parmesan cheese, if desired

Betty's Tips

If you'd like to serve six, this is an easy recipe to stretch. Add more veggies, such as broccoli flowerets or sliced carrots, and more pasta, too. For interest, use a different shape or color of pasta.

1. Cook and drain pasta as directed on package.

2. While pasta is cooking, spray 12-inch skillet with cooking spray and heat over medium heat. Cook asparagus, onions and 1 cup of the broth in skillet 5 to 7 minutes, stirring occasionally, until liquid has evaporated. Remove mixture from skillet.

3. Spray skillet with cooking spray and heat over medium-high heat. Add chicken and stir-fry about 5 minutes or until no longer pink in center.

4. Return asparagus mixture to skillet. Stir in remaining ½ cup broth, the basil, tomatoes, pepper and pasta. Cook about 2 minutes, stirring frequently, until mixture is hot. Sprinkle with cheese if desired.

1 serving: Calories 290 (Calories from Fat 45); Fat 5g (Saturated 1g); Cholesterol 70mg; Sodium 510mg; Carbohydrate 31g (Dietary Fiber 3g); Protein 33g

Chicken Pasta Primavera

4 SERVINGS PREP TIME: **10 MINUTES** START TO FINISH: **20 MINUTES**

8 ounces uncooked fettuccine

2 cups broccoli flowerets

1 medium carrot, thinly sliced

1 teaspoon olive or vegetable oil

1 pound boneless, skinless chicken breasts, cut into ½-inch strips

⅔ cup fat-free ranch dressing

¼ cup grated Parmesan cheese

¼ teaspoon garlic powder

¼ teaspoon dried basil leaves

SPEED SUPPER
Using leftover cooked chicken or purchased cooked chicken strips shaves cooking time.

1. Cook fettuccine as directed on package, except add broccoli and carrot 2 minutes before pasta is done. Drain and return to pan.

2. While pasta and vegetables are cooking, heat oil in 10-inch nonstick skillet over medium-high heat. Cook chicken in oil 2 to 3 minutes, stirring frequently, until chicken is no longer pink in center.

3. Add chicken and remaining ingredients to cooked fettuccine and vegetables. Toss until fettuccine is evenly coated with dressing.

1 serving: Calories 444 (Calories from Fat 48); Fat 5g (Saturated 2g); Cholesterol 71 mg; Sodium 645 mg; Carbohydrate 60g (Dietary Fiber 4g); Protein 38g

Shanghai Chicken and Noodles

6 SERVINGS PREP TIME: **20 MINUTES** START TO FINISH: **30 MINUTES**

1 pound boneless, skinless chicken breasts

8 ounces uncooked fettuccine

1 bag (1 pound) fresh or frozen stir-fry vegetables

1 cup sliced mushrooms (3 ounces)

¼ cup hoisin sauce

Betty's Tip

Hoisin sauce is a sweet, medium-spicy, thick, reddish-brown sauce made from soybeans, vinegar, chilies, spices and garlic. It is used in cooking and as a condiment. Look for it in the Asian foods section in your supermarket. Sorry, there's no substitute.

1. Remove fat from chicken. Cut chicken into ¼-inch slices. Cook and drain fettuccine as directed on package, except omit salt.

2. While pasta is cooking, spray nonstick wok or 12-inch nonstick skillet with cooking spray and heat over medium-high heat. Add chicken and stir-fry 3 to 4 minutes or until brown and no longer pink in center. Add vegetables and mushrooms. Stir-fry about 3 minutes or until vegetables are crisp-tender.

3. Stir in hoisin sauce. Heat to boiling, stirring constantly. Boil and stir 1 minute. Add fettuccine and toss until well coated and heated through.

1 serving: Calories 250 (Calories from Fat 35); Fat 4g (Saturated 1g); Cholesterol 75mg; Sodium 55mg; Carbohydrate 34g (Dietary Fiber 2g); Protein 22g

MAKE IT A MEAL

A chilled bowlful of mixed tropical fruits goes well with this Asian main dish. Toss cut-up pineapple, mango, bananas, lime juice and a sprinkling of brown sugar. Refrigerate during supper. Toss and serve with shredded coconut if desired.

Szechuan Chicken and Pasta

4 SERVINGS PREP TIME: **5 MINUTES** START TO FINISH: **30 MINUTES**

1 pound boneless, skinless chicken breasts, cut into ¾- to 1-inch pieces

1 medium onion, cut into thin wedges

2 cups water

1½ cups uncooked fusilli (corkscrew) pasta (3 ounces)

1 bag (1 pound 5 ounces) frozen Szechuan stir-fry mix with vegetables, Szechuan sauce and peanuts

SPEED SUPPER

For an additional time-saver, look for thinly presliced chicken breast strips in the meat aisle (the package may be labeled "chicken for stir-fry"). You'll need about 1 pound of strips for this recipe.

1. Spray 12-inch nonstick skillet with cooking spray and heat over medium-high heat. Add chicken and onion. Stir-fry 3 to 5 minutes or until chicken is light brown.

2. Stir in water and heat to boiling. Stir in pasta. Cook 8 to 10 minutes, stirring occasionally, until pasta is almost tender (do not drain).

3. Stir in Sauce Mix from stir-fry mix until well blended. Stir in Vegetables from stir-fry mix. Reduce heat to medium. Cover and cook 8 to 9 minutes, stirring occasionally, until vegetables are crisp-tender. Sprinkle with Peanuts from stir-fry mix.

1 serving: Calories 380 (Calories from Fat 90); Fat 10g (Saturated 2g); Cholesterol 50mg; Sodium 620mg; Carbohydrate 49g (Dietary Fiber 7g); Protein 30g

Pork Lo Mein

4 SERVINGS PREP TIME: **15 MINUTES** START TO FINISH: **25 MINUTES**

½ pound boneless pork loin

2½ cups snap pea pods

1½ cups baby carrots, cut lengthwise into
  ¼-inch sticks

½ package (9-ounce size) refrigerated linguine,
  cut into 2-inch pieces

⅓ cup chicken broth

1 tablespoon soy sauce

2 teaspoons cornstarch

1 teaspoon sugar

2 teaspoons finely chopped gingerroot

2 to 4 cloves garlic, finely chopped

2 teaspoons canola oil

½ cup thinly sliced red onion

  Toasted sesame seed, if desired

SPEED SUPPER
Fresh gingerroot adds such spunk to foods—it really livens up the flavor! If you don't use gingerroot often but like to keep it on hand, store it tightly wrapped in the freezer. To use, just peel off the thin brown skin and grate the amount you need.

1. Trim fat from pork. Cut pork with grain into 2 × 1-inch strips, then cut strips across grain into ⅛-inch slices. (Pork is easier to cut if partially frozen, about 1½ hours.) Remove strings from pea pods.

2. Heat 2 quarts water to boiling in 3-quart saucepan. Add pea pods, carrots and linguine; heat to boiling. Boil 2 to 3 minutes or just until linguine is tender; drain.

3. Mix broth, soy sauce, cornstarch, sugar, gingerroot and garlic in small bowl.

4. Heat oil in 12-inch nonstick skillet or wok over medium-high heat. Stir-fry pork and onion about 2 minutes or until pork is no longer pink. Stir broth mixture and add to pork mixture. Stir in pea pods, carrots and linguine. Cook 2 minutes, stirring occasionally. Sprinkle with sesame seed if desired.

1 serving: Calories 200 (Calories from Fat 45); Fat 5g (Saturated 1g); Cholesterol 35mg; Sodium 370mg; Carbohydrate 21g (Dietary Fiber 4g); Protein 17g

Creamy Bow-Ties with Ham and Vegetables

4 SERVINGS PREP TIME: **10 MINUTES** START TO FINISH: **25 MINUTES**

2 cups uncooked farfalle (bow-tie) pasta or wide egg noodles (4 ounces)

½ cup soft cream cheese with chives and onion

¾ cup half-and-half

1 cup baby carrots, cut lengthwise in half if large

8 ounces asparagus, cut into 1½-inch pieces

1½ cups fully cooked ham strips (1 × ¼ inch)

¼ teaspoon dried marjoram leaves

SPEED SUPPER
To save time, use frozen asparagus cuts.

1. Cook and drain pasta as directed on package.

2. While pasta is cooking, mix cream cheese and half-and-half in 12-inch nonstick skillet. Cook over medium heat 2 to 3 minutes, stirring constantly, until melted and smooth.

3. Stir in carrots. Cook 4 minutes, stirring occasionally. Stir in asparagus. Cover and cook 4 to 5 minutes, stirring occasionally, until vegetables are crisp-tender.

4. Stir in ham, marjoram and pasta. Cook, stirring occasionally, just until hot.

1 serving: Calories 425 (Calories from Fat 180); Fat 20g (Saturated 11g); Cholesterol 75mg; Sodium 860mg; Carbohydrate 40g (Dietary Fiber 3g); Protein 21g

Ravioli with Tomato-Alfredo Sauce

6 SERVINGS PREP TIME: **10 MINUTES** START TO FINISH: **20 MINUTES**

2 packages (9 ounces each) refrigerated sun-dried tomato- or cheese-filled ravioli

1 package (8 ounces) sliced mushrooms (3 cups)

1 large onion, coarsely chopped (1 cup)

1 jar (24 to 28 ounces) fat-free tomato pasta sauce (any variety)

½ cup fat-free half-and-half or refrigerated fat-free nondairy liquid creamer

¼ cup grated Parmesan cheese

¼ cup chopped fresh parsley

1. Cook and drain ravioli as directed on package; keep warm.

2. Spray same saucepan with cooking spray and heat over medium heat. Cook mushrooms and onion about 5 minutes, stirring frequently, until onion is crisp-tender.

3. Stir in pasta sauce and half-and-half. Heat to boiling; reduce heat. Stir in ravioli, cheese and parsley.

1 serving: Calories 225 (Calories from Fat 65); Fat 7g (Saturated 4g); Cholesterol 85mg; Sodium 1,100mg; Carbohydrate 30g (Dietary Fiber 2g); Protein 12g

MAKE IT A MEAL
Herbed Broccoli

4 SERVINGS PREP TIME: **8 MINUTES** START TO FINISH: **20 MINUTES**

1 pound broccoli, cut into 1-inch pieces

2 tablespoons olive or vegetable oil

1 teaspoon chopped fresh or ¼ teaspoon dried basil leaves

1 teaspoon chopped fresh or ¼ teaspoon dried oregano leaves

½ teaspoon salt

1 clove garlic, finely chopped

2 medium roma (plum) tomatoes, chopped (⅔ cup)

1. Heat 1 inch water (salted if desired) to boiling in 3-quart saucepan. Add broccoli. Cover and heat to boiling; reduce heat. Simmer about 10 minutes or until crisp-tender; drain.

2. Heat oil in 10-inch skillet over medium heat. Add basil, oregano, salt, garlic and tomatoes. Cook about 1 minute, stirring frequently, until hot. Pour over broccoli and toss.

1 serving: Calories 105 (Calories from Fat 64); Fat 7g (Saturated 1g); Cholesterol 0mg; Sodium 330mg; Carbohydrate 9g (Dietary Fiber 3g); Protein 4g

SPEED SUPPER

2 packages (10 ounces each) frozen chopped broccoli can be substituted for the fresh broccoli.

Baked Ziti and Bean Casserole

6 SERVINGS PREP TIME: **15 MINUTES** START TO FINISH: **30 MINUTES**

1 can (28 ounces) whole tomatoes, drained

1 cup fat-free ricotta cheese

¼ cup chopped red onion

1 tablespoon chopped fresh parsley

1 tablespoon chopped fresh or 1 teaspoon dried thyme leaves

½ teaspoon salt

¼ teaspoon crushed red pepper

4 cups hot cooked ziti or penne pasta

1 can (15 to 16 ounces) great northern beans, rinsed and drained

3 slices part-skim mozzarella cheese, about 6½ × 4 inches

Grated Parmesan cheese, if desired

1. Heat oven to 400°. Spray rectangular baking dish, 11 × 7 × 1½ inches, with cooking spray. Break up tomatoes in large bowl. Stir in ricotta cheese, onion, parsley, thyme, salt and red pepper. Carefully fold in pasta and beans.

2. Spread pasta mixture in baking dish. Arrange mozzarella cheese on top. Bake uncovered about 30 minutes or until mixture is hot and cheese is golden brown. Sprinkle with Parmesan cheese if desired.

1 serving: Calories 325 (Calories from Fat 55); Fat 6g (Saturated 4g); Cholesterol 15mg; Sodium 580mg; Carbohydrate 50g (Dietary Fiber 6g); Protein 24g

MAKE IT A MEAL

After such a rich and satisfying supper, finish with refreshing navel oranges, clementines, or tangerines.

Portabella Stroganoff

4 SERVINGS PREP TIME: **10 MINUTES** START TO FINISH: **20 MINUTES**

4 cups uncooked cholesterol-free noodles (8 ounces)

1 tablespoon margarine

¾ pound fresh portabella mushrooms, cut into 2 × ½-inch strips

1 medium onion, chopped (½ cup)

1 clove garlic, finely chopped

¾ cup beef broth

2 tablespoons ketchup

½ cup reduced-fat sour cream

Dash of pepper

Chopped fresh parsley, if desired

1. Cook and drain noodles as directed on package, except omit salt.

2. While noodles are cooking, melt margarine in 12-inch nonstick skillet over medium heat. Cook mushrooms, onion and garlic in margarine, stirring occasionally, until mushrooms are brown and tender.

3. Stir broth and ketchup into mushroom mixture. Cook 5 minutes, stirring occasionally. Stir in sour cream. Serve over noodles. Sprinkle with pepper and parsley if desired.

1 serving: Calories 215 (Calories from Fat 25); Fat 3g (Saturated 0g); Cholesterol 0mg; Sodium 280mg; Carbohydrate 40g (Dietary Fiber 3g); Protein 10g

MAKE IT A MEAL

Serve a salad on the side, made with crisp red-leaf romaine lettuce, shredded carrots and shredded red-skinned apples. Toss with bottled poppy seed dressing.

Noodles and Peanut Sauce Salad Bowl

4 SERVINGS PREP TIME: **10 MINUTES** START TO FINISH: **25 MINUTES**

8 ounces uncooked whole wheat linguine, broken in half

2 cups broccoli flowerets

1 cup julienne-cut carrots

1 medium bell pepper, cut into bite-size pieces

2 tablespoons water

2 teaspoons canola oil

¼ cup peanut butter

2 tablespoons rice vinegar or white vinegar

2 tablespoons reduced-sodium soy sauce

½ teaspoon ground ginger

⅛ teaspoon ground red pepper (cayenne)

3 medium green onions, chopped (3 tablespoons)

3 tablespoons chopped fresh cilantro

1. Cook linguine as directed on package, adding broccoli, carrots and bell pepper during the last minute of cooking. Drain pasta and vegetables. Rinse with cold water until pasta and vegetables are cool; drain.

2. Gradually beat water and oil into peanut butter with wire whisk in small bowl until smooth. Beat in vinegar, soy sauce, ginger and red pepper.

3. Stir together pasta mixture, peanut sauce, onions and cilantro in large serving bowl until well mixed.

1 serving: Calories 390 (Calories from Fat 90); Fat 10g (Saturated 1.5g); Cholesterol 0mg; Sodium 630mg; Carbohydrate 62g (Dietary Fiber 7g); Protein 15g

SPEED SUPPER

This dinner comes together really quickly if you replace the ingredients used in step 2 (water, oil, peanut butter, vinegar, soy sauce, ginger, and red pepper) with ¾ cup bottled Thai peanut sauce.

Whole Wheat Spaghetti with Spicy Eggplant Sauce

4 SERVINGS PREP TIME: **10 MINUTES** START TO FINISH: **25 MINUTES**

8 ounces uncooked whole wheat spaghetti

1 small eggplant, peeled and cubed

1 can (14½ ounces) Italian-style stewed tomatoes, undrained

1 can (8 ounces) tomato sauce

½ teaspoon crushed red pepper

2 tablespoons chopped fresh parsley or 2 teaspoons parsley flakes

1. Cook and drain spaghetti as directed on package.

2. While pasta is cooking, heat eggplant, stewed tomatoes, tomato sauce and red pepper in 10-inch skillet to boiling, stirring occasionally; reduce heat. Simmer uncovered about 15 minutes or until eggplant is tender. Stir in parsley. Serve over spaghetti.

1 serving: Calories 255 (Calories from Fat 10); Fat 1g (Saturated 0g); Cholesterol 0mg; Sodium 630mg; Carbohydrate 62g (Dietary Fiber 9g); Protein 11g

MAKE IT A MEAL

Make supper salads more fun by bypassing the salad bowl and putting out crudités and dip instead. Purchase baby-cut carrots, celery sticks and other favorite raw veggies and pair with your favorite dip instead of salad dressing.

Tuna Marinara with Linguine

6 SERVINGS PREP TIME: **15 MINUTES** START TO FINISH: **35 MINUTES**

8 ounces uncooked linguine

¾ cup tomato puree

¾ cup white wine or apple juice

2 cloves garlic, finely chopped

1 teaspoon olive or vegetable oil

1 can (14½ ounces) whole tomatoes, undrained

1 pound yellowfin tuna, cut into 1-inch pieces

3 tablespoons chopped fresh basil leaves

1 teaspoon grated lemon peel

2 tablespoons lemon juice

2 teaspoons capers

¼ teaspoon pepper

1. Cook and drain linguine as directed on package, except omit salt.

2. While pasta is cooking, cook tomato puree, wine, garlic, oil and tomatoes in 2-quart saucepan over medium heat 10 minutes, breaking up tomatoes and stirring occasionally.

3. Stir in fish. Cover and simmer about 7 minutes or until fish flakes easily with fork. Stir in linguine and remaining ingredients.

1 serving: Calories 275 (Calories from Fat 45); Fat 5g (Saturated 2g); Cholesterol 30mg; Sodium 290mg; Carbohydrate 37g (Dietary Fiber 3g); Protein 24g

MAKE IT A MEAL
Summer Squash Sauté

4 SERVINGS PREP TIME: **8 MINUTES** START TO FINISH: **15 MINUTES**

1 teaspoon olive or vegetable oil

½ cup chopped red onion

1 clove garlic, finely chopped

2½ cups coarsely chopped or sliced yellow summer squash or zucchini (about **2 medium**)

1 tablespoon balsamic or white wine vinegar

2 medium tomatoes, coarsely chopped (1½ cups)

2 tablespoons chopped fresh basil leaves

⅛ teaspoon salt

Dash of pepper

1. Heat oil in 8-inch skillet over medium heat. Cook onion and garlic in oil about 2 minutes, stirring occasionally, until onion is tender.

2. Stir in squash and vinegar. Cook about 3 minutes, stirring occasionally, until squash is crisp-tender. Stir in tomatoes. Cook about 2 minutes, stirring frequently, until tomatoes are heated through.

3. Stir in remaining ingredients.

1 serving: Calories 47 (Calories from Fat 13); Fat 1g (Saturated 0g); Cholesterol 0mg; Sodium 80mg; Carbohydrate 8g (Dietary Fiber 2g); Protein 2g

Broccoli-Cheese Calzones

6 SERVINGS PREP TIME: **15 MINUTES** START TO FINISH: **40 MINUTES**

1 container (15 ounces) fat-free ricotta cheese

1 package (10 ounces) frozen chopped broccoli, thawed

⅓ cup grated Parmesan cheese

¼ cup fat-free cholesterol-free egg product or 2 egg whites

1 teaspoon dried basil leaves

¼ teaspoon garlic powder

1 loaf (1 pound) frozen honey-wheat or white bread dough, thawed

1 can (8 ounces) pizza sauce

1. Heat oven to 375°. Grease 2 cookie sheets. Mix all ingredients except bread dough and pizza sauce.

2. Divide bread dough into 6 equal parts. Roll each part into 7-inch circle on lightly floured surface with floured rolling pin. Top half of each dough circle with cheese mixture to within 1 inch of edge. Carefully fold dough over filling. Pinch edge or press with fork to seal securely.

3. Place calzones on cookie sheets. Bake about 20 minutes or until golden brown. Cool 5 minutes.

4. While calzones are cooling, heat pizza sauce in 1-quart saucepan over medium heat about 2 minutes, stirring occasionally, until heated through. Spoon warm sauce over calzones.

1 serving: Calories 295 (Calories from Fat 35); Fat 4g (Saturated 2g); Cholesterol 5mg; Sodium 750mg; Carbohydrate 48g (Dietary Fiber 4g); Protein 21g

Red Pepper–Artichoke Pizza

4 SERVINGS PREP TIME: **10 MINUTES** START TO FINISH: **25 MINUTES**

1 can (10 ounces) refrigerated pizza crust dough

1 tablespoon fat-free (skim) milk

½ teaspoon garlic powder

½ teaspoon dried basil leaves

1 tub (8 ounces) reduced-fat cream cheese

1 jar (12 ounces) roasted red bell peppers, drained and coarsely chopped

1 jar (6 to 7 ounces) marinated artichoke hearts, drained and coarsely chopped

1 small tomato, chopped (½ cup)

3 medium green onions, sliced (3 tablespoons)

1. Heat oven to 425°. Grease cookie sheet. Pat pizza dough into 13 × 11-inch rectangle on cookie sheet. Bake about 5 minutes or until crust just starts to brown.

2. Mix milk, garlic powder, basil and cream cheese. Spread on partially baked crust. Top with bell peppers, artichoke hearts, tomato and onions.

3. Bake about 10 minutes or until vegetables are heated through and edges of crust are golden brown.

1 serving: Calories 335 (Calories from Fat 100); Fat 11g (Saturated 6g); Cholesterol 30mg; Sodium 740mg; Carbohydrate 51g (Dietary Fiber 5g); Protein 13g

Betty's Tip

If you have a little more time, try using your favorite homemade pizza crust instead of the refrigerated pizza dough.

Indian Curried Turkey Pizzas

4 SERVINGS PREP TIME: **6 MINUTES** START TO FINISH: **18 MINUTES**

4 pita bread folds or regular pita breads (6 inches in diameter)

½ cup mayonnaise or salad dressing

1 teaspoon curry powder

⅔ cup frozen green peas

3 cups shredded mozzarella cheese (12 ounces)

¼ pound thinly sliced deli turkey breast, cut into strips

1 large tomato, chopped (1 cup)

¼ cup bacon flavor bits or chips

1. Heat oven to 400°. Place pita breads on ungreased cookie sheet. Mix mayonnaise and curry powder. Spread evenly over pitas.

2. Rinse peas with cold water to separate; drain. Sprinkle ¼ cup of the cheese over each pita. Top with peas, turkey, tomato and bacon bits. Top with remaining cheese.

3. Bake 10 to 12 minutes or until cheese is melted.

1 serving: Calories 704 (Calories from Fat 393); Fat 44g (Saturated 14g); Cholesterol 88mg; Sodium 1,499mg; Carbohydrate 45g (Dietary Fiber 4g); Protein 33g

Betty's Tip

Pita bread makes an excellent crust for single-serving pizzas. Experiment with a variety of toppings, such as those suggested in this recipe.

Ranchero Beef Pizza

6 SERVINGS PREP TIME: **5 MINUTES** START TO FINISH: **25 MINUTES**

1 package (16 ounces) ready-to-serve original Italian pizza crust (12 inches in diameter)

3 cups shredded smoked or regular Cheddar cheese (12 ounces)

1 pound cooked barbecued beef

4 slices red onion, separated into rings

1. Heat oven to 400°.

2. Place pizza crust on ungreased cookie sheet. Sprinkle with 1 cup of the cheese. Top with beef and onion. Sprinkle with remaining 2 cups cheese. Bake 15 to 20 minutes or until hot.

1 serving: Calories 545 (Calories from Fat 235); Fat 26g (Saturated 15g); Cholesterol 88mg; Sodium 1,150mg; Carbohydrate 48g (Dietary Fiber 0g); Protein 30g

SPEED SUPPER

Fully cooked and sliced barbecued beef is now available in the refrigerated meat section or deli of most grocery stores. If the slices of meat are large, cut them into small chunks before placing on top of the pizza.

Canadian Bacon Whole Wheat Pizza

8 SERVINGS PREP TIME: 15 MINUTES START TO FINISH: 55 MINUTES

1 package regular or quick active dry yeast

1 cup warm water (105°F to 115°F)

2½ cups whole wheat flour

2 tablespoons olive oil

½ teaspoon salt

1 tablespoon olive oil

1 tablespoon yellow cornmeal

1 can (8 ounces) pizza sauce

2 cups finely shredded Italian-style mozzarella and Parmesan cheese blend (8 ounces)

1 package (6 ounces) sliced Canadian-style bacon, cut into fourths

1 small green bell pepper, chopped (½ cup)

1. Dissolve yeast in warm water in medium bowl. Stir in flour, 2 tablespoons oil and the salt. Beat vigorously with spoon 20 strokes. Let dough rest 20 minutes.

2. Move oven rack to lowest position. Heat oven to 425°. Grease cookie sheet with 1 tablespoon oil and sprinkle with cornmeal. Pat dough into 12 × 10-inch rectangle on cookie sheet, using floured fingers. Pinch edges to form ½-inch rim.

3. Spread pizza sauce over crust. Top with cheese, bacon and bell pepper. Bake 15 to 20 minutes or until edge of crust is golden brown.

1 serving: Calories 320 (Calories from Fat 130); Fat 14g (Saturated 6g); Cholesterol 35mg; Sodium 750mg; Carbohydrate 32g (Dietary Fiber 5g); Protein 16g

Betty's Tip

A whole wheat pizza crust makes a great base for the family-friendly Canadian-style bacon and cheese toppings. Vary the flavor by using different toppings, such as pepperoni, cooked and drained ground beef, vegetables and different types of cheese.

Vegetable Stew with Polenta

4 SERVINGS PREP TIME: **20 MINUTES** START TO FINISH: **1 HOUR 15 MINUTES**

1 tablespoon olive oil

1 medium onion, coarsely chopped (½ cup)

1 medium yellow or green bell pepper, coarsely chopped (1 cup)

4 cloves garlic, finely chopped

2 medium carrots, cut into ¼-inch slices (1 cup)

2 cans (14½ ounces each) diced tomatoes with basil, garlic and oregano, undrained

1 can (15 to 16 ounces) black-eyed peas, rinsed and drained

1 can (19 ounces) cannellini beans, rinsed and drained

1 cup water

1 teaspoon Italian seasoning

¼ teaspoon pepper

1 tube (16 ounces) refrigerated polenta

1 cup frozen cut green beans

1. In 4½- to 5-quart Dutch oven, heat oil over medium heat. Cook onion, bell pepper and garlic in oil 5 to 6 minutes, stirring frequently, until onion is softened.

2. Stir in remaining ingredients except polenta and green beans. Heat to boiling, then reduce heat to medium-low. Cover and cook 35 to 40 minutes, stirring occasionally, until carrots are tender and stew is hot. Meanwhile, cook polenta as directed; keep warm.

3. Stir frozen green beans into stew. Cover and cook 5 to 6 minutes, stirring occasionally, until beans are hot. To serve, spoon stew over polenta.

1 serving: Calories 460 (Calories from Fat 45); Fat 5g (Saturated 1g); Cholesterol 0mg; Sodium 790mg; Carbohydrate 81g (Dietary Fiber 16g); Protein 23g

SPEED SUPPER
Tubes of refrigerated polenta can be found in the produce section of the supermarket.

Barley-Chicken Medley

4 SERVINGS PREP TIME: **10 MINUTES** START TO FINISH: **25 MINUTES**

½ pound boneless, skinless chicken breasts

2 cups chicken broth

1 cup uncooked quick-cooking barley

½ teaspoon dried dill weed

½ teaspoon garlic salt

2 teaspoons vegetable oil

2½ cups thinly sliced zucchini or carrot

1 medium onion, cut lengthwise in half, then cut crosswise into thin slices

1. Remove fat from chicken. Cut chicken into ¾-inch pieces. Heat broth to boiling in 1½-quart saucepan. Stir in barley, dill weed and garlic salt; reduce heat to low. Cover and simmer about 10 minutes or until barley is tender; remove from heat. Let stand covered 5 minutes.

2. While barley is cooking, spray 10-inch nonstick skillet with cooking spray and heat over medium-high heat. Stir-fry chicken about 4 minutes or until no longer pink in center. Remove chicken from skillet; keep warm.

3. Add oil to skillet and rotate skillet to coat with oil. Add zucchini and onion. Stir-fry about 4 minutes or until vegetables are crisp-tender. Stir in chicken. Toss with cooked barley.

1 serving: Calories 320 (Calories from Fat 65); Fat 7g (Saturated 2g); Cholesterol 55mg; Sodium 700mg; Carbohydrate 44g (Dietary Fiber 9g); Protein 29g

MAKE IT A MEAL
Zesty Salsa Corn

5 SERVINGS PREP TIME: **5 MINUTES** START TO FINISH: **10 MINUTES**

1 bag (1 pound) frozen whole kernel corn

½ cup salsa

¼ cup sliced ripe olives

Cook corn as directed on package. Stir in salsa and olives and cook until hot.

1 serving: Calories 85 (Calories from Fat 10); Fat 1g (Saturated 0g); Cholesterol 0mg; Sodium 130mg; Carbohydrate 19g (Dietary Fiber 3g); Protein 3g

Italian Turkey-Couscous Salad

6 SERVINGS PREP TIME: 15 MINUTES START TO FINISH: 15 MINUTES

2 cups chicken broth

1⅓ cups uncooked couscous

1 bag (1 pound) frozen broccoli, carrots, onions, red peppers, celery, water chestnuts and mushrooms, thawed

3 cups cubed cooked turkey or chicken

¾ cup fat-free creamy Italian dressing

Lettuce leaves, if desired

1. Heat broth to boiling in 1½-quart saucepan; reduce heat. Stir in couscous and remove from heat. Cover and let stand 5 minutes.

2. Mix couscous, vegetables and turkey in large bowl. Pour dressing over mixture and toss lightly to coat. Line 6 salad plates with lettuce, if desired, and spoon salad onto lettuce.

1 serving: Calories 300 (Calories from Fat 55); Fat 6g (Saturated 2g); Cholesterol 60mg; Sodium 620mg; Carbohydrate 38g (Dietary Fiber 4g); Protein 27g

Spiced Chicken and Apricot Couscous

6 SERVINGS PREP TIME: **10 MINUTES** START TO FINISH: **25 MINUTES**

2 tablespoons olive or vegetable oil

1 pound boneless, skinless chicken breasts, cut into 1-inch pieces

1 cup dried apricots, cut up

1¼ teaspoons ground cinnamon

¼ teaspoon ground allspice

1 can (14½ ounces) chicken broth

¾ cup uncooked couscous

1 cup sliced almonds

3 tablespoons chopped fresh basil leaves

1. Heat oil in 12-inch skillet over medium-high heat. Cook chicken in oil, stirring frequently, until brown.

2. Stir in apricots, cinnamon, allspice and broth. Heat to boiling.

3. Stir in couscous and remove from heat. Cover and let stand about 5 minutes or until liquid is absorbed. Add almonds and basil and toss gently.

1 serving: Calories 310 (Calories from Fat 125); Fat 14g (Saturated 2g); Cholesterol 44mg; Sodium 362mg; Carbohydrate 21g (Dietary Fiber 3g); Protein 24g

SPEED SUPPER
Use your kitchen scissors to quickly cut up the apricots for this recipe.

MAKE IT A MEAL
Serve with a salad of sliced cucumber and chopped tomato and a dressing of plain yogurt spiked with crushed red pepper and chopped fresh mint.

Spanish Rice Bake

4 SERVINGS PREP TIME: **20 MINUTES** START TO FINISH: **1 HOUR 25 MINUTES**

2 tablespoons canola oil

1 cup uncooked brown long-grain rice

1 medium onion, chopped (½ cup)

1 small green bell pepper, chopped (½ cup)

1 cup frozen whole kernel corn, thawed, drained

1 can (10¾ ounces) condensed tomato soup

2½ cups boiling water

1 tablespoon chopped fresh cilantro, if desired

1 teaspoon chili powder

¼ teaspoon salt

1½ cups shredded reduced-fat Colby-Monterey Jack cheese (6 ounces)

Betty's Tip

Meat lovers can stir in their favorite cooked meat with the rice mixture; use a 3-quart casserole. Cooked ground beef, diced pepperoni, crumbled cooked bacon or cooked sausage works well.

1. Heat oven to 375°. Spray 2-quart casserole with cooking spray. Heat oil in 10-inch skillet over medium heat. Cook brown rice, onion and bell pepper in oil 6 to 8 minutes, stirring frequently, until rice is light brown and onion is tender. Stir in corn.

2. Mix remaining ingredients except cheese in casserole. Stir in rice mixture and 1 cup of the cheese.

3. Cover and bake 20 minutes. Stir mixture. Cover and bake about 30 minutes longer or until rice is tender. Stir mixture and sprinkle with remaining ½ cup cheese. Bake uncovered 2 to 3 minutes or until cheese is melted. Let stand 10 minutes before serving.

1 serving: Calories 460 (Calories from Fat 160); Fat 18g (Saturated 6g); Cholesterol 20mg; Sodium 960mg; Carbohydrate 59g (Dietary Fiber 8g); Protein 17g

CHAPTER 2

Easy Egg and Cheese Meals

Cheesy Scrambled Eggs

4 SERVINGS PREP TIME: **10 MINUTES** START TO FINISH: **20 MINUTES**

1½ cups fat-free cholesterol-free egg product

¼ cup fat-free (skim) milk

½ teaspoon salt

¼ teaspoon red pepper sauce

1 small green bell pepper, chopped (½ cup)

½ package (8-ounce size) reduced-fat cream cheese (Neufchâtel), softened

4 English muffins, split and toasted

½ cup shredded reduced-fat Cheddar cheese (2 ounces)

Paprika, if desired

1. Mix egg product, milk, salt and pepper sauce; set aside.

2. Spray 10-inch nonstick skillet with cooking spray and heat over medium heat. Cook bell pepper in skillet about 5 minutes, stirring frequently, until tender. Pour egg product mixture into skillet. As mixture begins to set on bottom and side, gently lift cooked portions with spatula so that thin, uncooked portion can flow to bottom. Avoid constant stirring. Cook about 3 minutes or until eggs are thickened throughout but still moist; remove from heat.

3. Spoon cream cheese over egg mixture. Gently stir cream cheese into eggs until cheese is smooth and melted. Spoon egg mixture over English muffin halves. Sprinkle with Cheddar cheese.

4. Set oven control to broil. Place English muffin halves on ungreased cookie sheet. Broil with tops 4 inches from heat about 2 minutes or just until cheese begins to melt. Sprinkle with paprika if desired.

1 serving: Calories 275 (Calories from Fat 80); Fat 9g (Saturated 5g); Cholesterol 25mg; Sodium 900mg; Carbohydrate 32g (Dietary Fiber 3g); Protein 19g

MAKE IT A MEAL

Cut up slices of fresh fruit and microwave some strips of bacon.

Scrambled Eggs Rancheros

4 SERVINGS PREP TIME: **10 MINUTES** START TO FINISH: **15 MINUTES**

4 fat-free flour tortillas (6 to 8 inches in diameter)

1 cup salsa

1½ cups fat-free cholesterol-free egg product

¼ cup fat-free (skim) milk

½ teaspoon onion salt

⅛ teaspoon pepper

2 teaspoons margarine

¾ cup shredded reduced-fat Cheddar cheese (3 ounces)

1. Heat tortillas as directed on package. Heat salsa in 1-quart saucepan over medium heat about 2 minutes, stirring occasionally, until heated through. Remove from heat and cover to keep warm.

2. While salsa is heating, mix egg product, milk, onion salt and pepper. Melt margarine in 10-inch nonstick skillet over medium heat. Pour egg product mixture into skillet. As mixture begins to set on bottom and side, gently lift cooked portions with spatula so that thin, uncooked portion can flow to bottom. Avoid constant stirring. Cook about 3 minutes or until eggs are thickened throughout but still moist.

3. Spread salsa over each tortilla. Divide scrambled eggs among tortillas. Sprinkle with cheese.

1 serving: Calories 210 (Calories from Fat 35); Fat 4g (Saturated 1g); Cholesterol 5mg; Sodium 990mg; Carbohydrate 30g (Dietary Fiber 3g); Protein 17g

MAKE IT A MEAL

Cut 2 red or yellow bell peppers and 1 medium red onion into thick slices. Fry in 2 tablespoons olive oil for about 10 minutes, stirring occasionally, or until crisp-tender. Season to taste with salt and black pepper.

Italian Frittata with Vinaigrette Tomatoes

5 SERVINGS PREP TIME: **10 MINUTES** START TO FINISH: **35 MINUTES**

1 can (14 ounces) chicken broth

¾ cup uncooked bulgur

1 medium zucchini, sliced, slices cut in half crosswise (1½ cups)

1 cup sliced mushrooms (3 ounces)

1 small red bell pepper, chopped (½ cup)

1 small onion, chopped (¼ cup)

½ teaspoon dried oregano leaves

½ teaspoon dried basil leaves

6 eggs

⅓ cup milk

¼ teaspoon salt

¼ teaspoon pepper

½ cup shredded mozzarella cheese (2 ounces)

3 medium roma (plum) tomatoes, chopped, drained (1 cup)

2 tablespoons balsamic vinaigrette dressing

Betty's Tip

Bulgur adds an extra chewiness and heartiness to this fantastic frittata, and kids love it! To substitute for the oregano and basil, you can use 1 teaspoon Italian seasoning.

1. Heat oven to 350°. Heat broth to boiling in 12-inch ovenproof nonstick skillet over high heat. Stir in bulgur and reduce heat to low. Top bulgur evenly with zucchini, mushrooms, bell pepper and onion. Sprinkle with oregano and basil. Cover and cook 12 minutes. Fluff bulgur with spatula, mixing with vegetables.

2. Meanwhile, beat eggs, milk, salt and pepper with wire whisk in medium bowl until well blended. Pour egg mixture evenly over bulgur mixture. Increase heat to medium-low. Cover and cook 5 minutes.

3. Remove cover and sprinkle with cheese. Bake uncovered 5 to 7 minutes or until sharp knife inserted in center of egg mixture comes out clean.

4. Meanwhile, mix tomatoes and dressing in medium microwavable bowl. Microwave uncovered on High 30 seconds to blend flavors.

5. Cut frittata into wedges (bulgur will form a "crust" on the bottom; use spatula to lift wedges out of skillet). Top with tomato mixture.

1 serving: Calories 264 (Calories from Fat 108); Fat 12g (Saturated 4g); Cholesterol 264mg; Sodium 684mg; Carbohydrate 24g (Dietary Fiber 5g); Protein 17g

Cheddar Strata with Onions

6 SERVINGS PREP TIME: **5 MINUTES** START TO FINISH: **1 HOUR 20 MINUTES**

1 teaspoon vegetable oil

2 medium onions, sliced

8 slices rye bread

2 tablespoons Dijon mustard

1½ cups shredded Cheddar cheese (6 ounces)

1 large tomato, seeded and coarsely chopped (1 cup)

1½ cups milk

4 eggs

SPEED SUPPER

This dish can be assembled and refrigerated up to 24 hours before baking. You may need to add 5 to 10 minutes to the bake time.

1. Heat oven to 300°. Spray square baking dish, 8 × 8 × 2 inches, with cooking spray.

2. Heat oil in 10-inch nonstick skillet over medium-high heat. Cook onions in oil 6 to 8 minutes, stirring frequently, until golden brown; remove from heat.

3. Trim crusts from bread. Spread mustard on one side of each bread slice. Arrange 4 slices, mustard sides up, in baking dish. Layer 1 cup of the cheese, the tomato and onions on bread. Place remaining bread, mustard sides down, on onions. Beat milk and eggs until well blended. Pour evenly over bread.

4. Bake uncovered about 1 hour or until center is set and bread is golden brown. Sprinkle with remaining ½ cup cheese. Let stand 10 minutes before cutting.

1 serving: Calories 280 (Calories from Fat 145); Fat 16g (Saturated 8g); Cholesterol 175mg; Sodium 490mg; Carbohydrate 21g (Dietary Fiber 3g); Protein 16g

MAKE IT A MEAL

Grab a bag of Oriental salad greens and top the salad with drained canned mandarin orange segments and toasted slivered almonds.

Tomato-Corn Quiche

6 SERVINGS PREP TIME: **10 MINUTES** START TO FINISH: **1 HOUR 5 MINUTES**

1 cup evaporated fat-free milk

½ cup fat-free cholesterol-free egg product

2 tablespoons all-purpose flour

1 tablespoon chopped fresh cilantro

½ teaspoon chili powder

¼ teaspoon onion powder

¼ teaspoon salt

¼ teaspoon pepper

1 cup frozen whole kernel corn, thawed

¾ cup shredded reduced-fat Cheddar cheese (3 ounces)

1 medium tomato, seeded and chopped (¾ cup)

1. Heat oven to 350°. Spray pie plate, 9 × 1¼ inches, with cooking spray. Mix all ingredients except corn, cheese and tomato in medium bowl until blended. Stir in remaining ingredients. Pour into pie plate.

2. Bake 35 to 45 minutes or until knife inserted in center comes out clean. Let stand 10 minutes before cutting.

1 serving: Calories 95 (Calories from Fat 10); Fat 1g (Saturated 1g); Cholesterol 5mg; Sodium 270mg; Carbohydrate 14g (Dietary Fiber 1g); Protein 9g

SPEED SUPPER

Using shelf-stable evaporated fat-free milk means you can prepare this supper without making a special trip to the supermarket for fresh cream.

MAKE IT A MEAL

While the quiche bakes, wash 1¼ pounds Swiss chard. Transfer to a colander to drain the excess water. Chop the stems and leaves coarsely. Place the wet leaves and stems in a 3-quart microwavable casserole. Cover and microwave on High 8 to 10 minutes, stirring after 5 minutes, until tender. Let stand covered 1 minute. Season to taste with salt and pepper. Drizzle with olive oil.

Tortilla Casserole

6 SERVINGS PREP TIME: 20 MINUTES START TO FINISH: 1 HOUR

1 can (15 to 16 ounces) kidney beans, drained

½ cup fat-free (skim) milk

¼ cup fat-free cholesterol-free egg product
or 2 egg whites

¼ cup chopped fresh cilantro

½ cup vegetable broth

1 large onion, chopped (1 cup)

1 medium green bell pepper, chopped (1 cup)

2 cloves garlic, finely chopped

2 cans (4 ounces each) chopped mild green
chilies, drained

4 cups reduced-fat tortilla chips

1 cup shredded reduced-fat Cheddar cheese
(4 ounces)

Spicy Fresh Chili Sauce (right)
or ¾ cup salsa

Reduced-fat sour cream, if desired

1. Heat oven to 375°. Spray 2-quart casserole with cooking spray.

2. Mash beans and milk in medium bowl until smooth. Stir in egg product and 2 tablespoons of the cilantro; reserve. (Or place beans, milk, egg product and 2 tablespoons of the cilantro in blender or food processor; cover and blend until smooth.)

3. Cook broth, onion, bell pepper, garlic and chilies in 10-inch nonstick skillet over medium heat about 5 minutes, stirring occasionally, until onion is tender. Stir in remaining 2 tablespoons cilantro.

4. Coarsely chop half of the tortilla chips. Place 1 cup of the chopped chips in bottom of casserole. Spread reserved bean mixture over chips. Spread vegetable mixture over bean mixture. Sprinkle with ½ cup of the cheese. Top with remaining chopped chips. Sprinkle with remaining ½ cup cheese.

5. Bake uncovered 30 to 35 minutes or until hot and cheese is golden brown. Serve with Spicy Fresh Chili Sauce, the remaining chips and sour cream if desired.

SPICY FRESH CHILI SAUCE

1 medium tomato, finely chopped (¾ cup)

3 medium green onions, sliced
(3 tablespoons)

1 medium jalapeño chili, seeded and finely
chopped (1 tablespoon)

1 clove garlic, finely chopped

1 tablespoon chopped fresh cilantro

¼ teaspoon ground cumin

Mix all ingredients. Serve immediately or refrigerate until serving.

1 serving: Calories 180 (Calories from Fat 20); Fat 2g
(Saturated 1g); Cholesterol 5mg; Sodium 460mg;
Carbohydrate 33g (Dietary Fiber 6g); Protein 13g

Egg-Asparagus Salad

4 SERVINGS PREP TIME: **10 MINUTES** START TO FINISH: **15 MINUTES**

Dijon Vinaigrette (right)

2 teaspoons vegetable oil

1 pound asparagus, cut into 2-inch pieces

1 medium red bell pepper, cut into 1-inch pieces

1 package (4 ounces) mixed baby greens

4 hard-cooked eggs, chopped

1 cup croutons

1. Prepare Dijon Vinaigrette.

2. Heat oil in 10-inch nonstick skillet over medium-high heat. Cook asparagus and bell pepper in oil about 5 minutes, stirring frequently, until crisp-tender.

3. Line large platter with baby greens. Top with cooked vegetables. Sprinkle with eggs and croutons. Drizzle with vinaigrette.

DIJON VINAIGRETTE

3 tablespoons vegetable oil

2 tablespoons red wine vinegar

1½ teaspoons sugar

1½ teaspoons Dijon mustard

½ teaspoon salt

⅛ teaspoon pepper

Shake all ingredients in tightly covered container.

1 serving: Calories 267 (Calories from Fat 165); Fat 19g (Saturated 4g); Cholesterol 212mg; Sodium 463mg; Carbohydrate 15g (Dietary Fiber 4g); Protein 10g

Betty's Tip

How do you get hard-cooked eggs without a green ring around the yolk? Place raw eggs in saucepan and add enough cold water just to cover eggs. Heat to boiling. Remove the saucepan from the heat. Cover the saucepan and let the eggs stand in the water 18 minutes. Immediately drain and rinse with cold water; peel.

MAKE IT A MEAL

Crusty whole grain bread is ideal with this hearty salad.

Potato, Egg and Sausage Frittata

4 SERVINGS PREP TIME: **10 MINUTES** START TO FINISH: **30 MINUTES**

4 eggs or 8 egg whites

¼ cup fat-free (skim) milk

1 teaspoon olive oil

1½ cups frozen country-style shredded hash brown potatoes (from 30-ounce bag)

4 frozen soy-protein breakfast sausage links (from 8-ounce box), cut into eighths

¼ teaspoon salt

⅛ teaspoon dried basil leaves

⅛ teaspoon dried oregano leaves

3 medium roma (plum) tomatoes, chopped (1 cup)

½ cup shredded mozzarella and Asiago cheese blend with garlic (2 ounces)

Freshly ground pepper, if desired

Betty's Tip

If you haven't tried the newest soy products lately, you're in for a pleasant surprise. Soy sausage is a tasty alternative to higher-fat regular sausage and an easy addition to this fresh-tasting frittata.

1. Beat eggs and milk with fork or wire whisk in small bowl until well blended; set aside.

2. Coat 10-inch nonstick skillet with oil and heat over medium heat. Cook potatoes and sausage links in oil 6 to 8 minutes, stirring occasionally, until potatoes are golden brown.

3. Pour egg mixture over potato mixture. Cook uncovered over medium-low heat about 5 minutes. As mixture begins to set on bottom and side, gently lift cooked portions with spatula so that thin, uncooked portion can flow to bottom. Avoid constant stirring. Cook until eggs are thickened throughout but still moist.

4. Sprinkle with salt, basil, oregano, tomatoes and cheese. Reduce heat to low. Cover; cook about 5 minutes or until center is set and cheese is melted. Sprinkle with pepper if desired.

1 serving: Calories 250 (Calories from Fat 110); Fat 12g (Saturated 4.5g); Cholesterol 220mg; Sodium 570mg; Carbohydrate 20g (Dietary Fiber 2g); Protein 17g

Spinach Soufflé

4 SERVINGS PREP TIME: **25 MINUTES** START TO FINISH: **1 HOUR**

1 package (9 ounces) frozen chopped spinach, thawed

3 tablespoons all-purpose flour

½ teaspoon dried dill weed

¼ teaspoon salt

¼ teaspoon pepper

1 cup milk

1 cup shredded Cheddar cheese (4 ounces)

5 large eggs

1. Heat oven to 350°. Grease bottom and side of 2-quart casserole with shortening.

2. Squeeze spinach to drain. Spread on paper towels and pat dry.

3. Mix flour, dill weed, salt, pepper and milk in 2-quart saucepan. Cook over medium-high heat, stirring constantly, until thickened; remove from heat. Stir in cheese and spinach.

4. Separate eggs and set egg whites aside. Beat egg yolks in large bowl with wire whisk. Gradually stir in spinach mixture. Beat egg whites in large bowl with electric mixer on high speed until stiff. Gently fold egg whites into egg yolk mixture.

5. Spoon spinach mixture into casserole. Bake uncovered 30 to 35 minutes or until golden brown and puffed.

1 serving: Calories 270 (Calories from Fat 155); Fat 17g (Saturated 9g); Cholesterol 300mg; Sodium 470mg; Carbohydrate 11g (Dietary Fiber 1g); Protein 19g

MAKE IT A MEAL
Broiled Parmesan Tomatoes

4 SERVINGS PREP TIME: **5 MINUTES** START TO FINISH: **17 MINUTES**

2 medium tomatoes

2 tablespoons mayonnaise or salad dressing

2 tablespoons grated Parmesan cheese

1 teaspoon chopped fresh or ¼ teaspoon dried basil leaves

1 teaspoon Dijon mustard

1. Heat oven to 350°.

2. Core tomatoes. Cut crosswise into ¾-inch slices. Place in single layer on rack in broiler pan.

3. Mix mayonnaise, 1 tablespoon of the cheese, the basil and mustard. Spread about 1 teaspoon of mixture over each tomato slice. Sprinkle 1 tablespoon remaining cheese over tomatoes. Bake about 8 minutes or until hot. Set oven control to broil. Broil tomatoes with tops 6 inches from heat 2 to 4 minutes or until topping is golden and bubbly.

1 serving: Calories 76 (Calories from Fat 57); Fat 6g (Saturated 1g); Cholesterol 5mg; Sodium 111mg; Carbohydrate 3g (Dietary Fiber 1g); Protein 2g

Pan-Roasted Garden Vegetables with Eggs

4 SERVINGS PREP TIME: **10 MINUTES** START TO FINISH: **25 MINUTES**

3 tablespoons olive or vegetable oil

1 cup sliced mushrooms (3 ounces)

½ medium onion, cut into wedges

1 package (1 pound 10 ounces) frozen roasted potatoes, broccoli, cauliflower and carrots with Parmesan and Romano seasonings

4 eggs

½ cup shredded Italian-style six-cheese blend (2 ounces)

Betty's Tip

Italian blend cheese is a packaged preshredded blend of six different cheeses: Asiago, Fontina, mozzarella, Parmesan, provolone and Romano. If you like, shredded Parmesan cheese can be used in place of the Italian blend cheese.

1. Heat oil in 12-inch nonstick skillet over medium-high heat. Add mushrooms, onion and frozen vegetables. Sprinkle with contents of seasoning packet from frozen vegetables and stir to coat vegetables. Cook 6 minutes, stirring occasionally.

2. Make 4 indentations in vegetable mixture. Break 1 egg into each indentation. Reduce heat to medium-low. Cover and cook 6 to 9 minutes or until egg whites and yolks are firm, not runny.

3. Sprinkle with cheese. Cover and cook about 1 minute or until cheese is melted.

1 serving: Calories 349 (Calories from Fat 167); Fat 19g (Saturated 5g); Cholesterol 222mg; Sodium 226mg; Carbohydrate 28g (Dietary Fiber 5g); Protein 14g

Vegetable–Cheddar Cheese Soup

8 SERVINGS PREP TIME: **10 MINUTES** START TO FINISH: **18 MINUTES**

½ cup margarine or butter

2 medium carrots, finely chopped

1 small onion, finely chopped (¼ cup)

1 medium stalk celery, finely chopped (½ cup)

2 medium zucchini, cut into 2-inch strips

½ cup all-purpose flour

1 teaspoon ground mustard

2 cups chicken broth

2 cups half-and-half

3 cups shredded Cheddar cheese (12 ounces)

1. Heat margarine in Dutch oven until melted. Cook carrots, onion and celery in margarine until softened. Stir in zucchini and cook about 2 minutes or until crisp-tender. Mix flour and mustard and stir into vegetable mixture.

2. Gradually stir in chicken broth and half-and-half. Cook over medium heat, stirring constantly until mixture boils; boil 1 minute. Slowly stir in cheese until melted.

1 serving: Calories 400 (Calories from Fat 295); Fat 33g (Saturated 15g); Cholesterol 65mg; Sodium 710mg; Carbohydrate 13g (Dietary Fiber 2g); Protein 15g

MAKE IT A MEAL

Serve hearty dark rye bread with this soup.

Cheese Enchiladas

4 SERVINGS PREP TIME: **15 MINUTES** START TO FINISH: **45 MINUTES**

2 cups shredded Monterey Jack cheese
(8 ounces)

1 medium onion, chopped (½ cup)

1¼ cups shredded Cheddar cheese (5 ounces)

½ cup sour cream

2 tablespoons chopped fresh parsley

¼ teaspoon pepper

1 small green bell pepper, chopped (½ cup)

1 clove garlic, finely chopped

1 can (15 ounces) tomato sauce

⅔ cup water

1 tablespoon chili powder

1½ teaspoons chopped fresh or ½ teaspoon
dried oregano leaves

¼ teaspoon ground cumin

8 corn tortillas (5 or 6 inches in diameter)

Chopped green onions, if desired

1. Heat oven to 350°.

2. Stir Monterey Jack cheese, onion, 1 cup of the Cheddar cheese, the sour cream, parsley and pepper in large bowl. Cover and set aside.

3. Place bell pepper, garlic, tomato sauce, water, chili powder, oregano, and cumin in 2-quart saucepan. Heat to boiling over medium heat, stirring occasionally. Reduce heat so that mixture bubbles gently. Cook uncovered 5 minutes. Pour enough of mixture into ungreased rectangular baking dish, 11 × 7 × 1½ inches, to cover bottom.

4. Place 2 tortillas between dampened microwavable paper towels or microwavable plastic wrap. Microwave on High 15 to 20 seconds to soften. Dip each tortilla into sauce mixture to coat both sides.

5. Spoon about ¼ cup of the Monterey Jack mixture down one side of each softened tortilla to within 1 inch of edge. Roll tortilla around filling and place, seam side down, in pan. Repeat with remaining tortillas and Monterey Jack mixture. Pour any remaining sauce over enchiladas. Sprinkle the remaining ¼ cup Cheddar cheese over enchiladas.

6. Bake uncovered about 20 minutes or until hot and bubbly. Garnish with additional sour cream and green onions if desired.

1 serving: Calories 565 (Calories from Fat 295); Fat 33g (Saturated 16g); Cholesterol 110mg; Sodium 1,000mg; Carbohydrate 39g (Dietary Fiber 6g); Protein 34g

SPEED SUPPER
To save time, replace the bell pepper, garlic, tomato sauce, water, chili powder, oregano and cumin with a 16-ounce jar of salsa.

MAKE IT A MEAL
Serve with grilled zucchini or yellow summer squash that's been brushed with a mixture of oil and chili powder.

Teriyaki Vegetable Medley with Eggs

4 SERVINGS PREP TIME: **8 MINUTES** START TO FINISH: **20 MINUTES**

1 bag (1 pound 5 ounces) frozen broccoli, snap peas, water chestnuts and red peppers with teriyaki sauce

2 tablespoons margarine or butter

8 eggs, beaten

SPEED SUPPER
Only three ingredients! This recipe takes advantage of the frozen vegetable mixtures now available that come with a separate sauce packet.

1. Cook vegetables and sauce in 10-inch nonstick skillet over medium heat about 7 minutes, stirring frequently, until vegetables are crisp-tender. Remove mixture from skillet; keep warm.

2. Melt margarine in same skillet over medium heat. Pour eggs into skillet. As eggs begin to set on bottom and side, gently lift cooked portions with spatula so that thin, uncooked portion can flow to bottom. Avoid constant stirring. Cook 4 to 5 minutes or until eggs are thickened throughout but still moist.

3. Top eggs with vegetable mixture. Cut into wedges to serve.

1 serving: Calories 270 (Calories from Fat 140); Fat 16g (Saturated 4g); Cholesterol 425mg; Sodium 484mg; Carbohydrate 19g (Dietary Fiber 3g); Protein 14g

MAKE IT A MEAL
Serve with fresh orange slices and toast.

Vegetable-Cheese Bake

6 SERVINGS PREP TIME: **10 MINUTES** START TO FINISH: **40 MINUTES**

8 slices soft whole wheat bread, cut into ½-inch cubes

2 cups shredded part-skim mozzarella cheese (8 ounces)

1½ cups frozen green peas or whole kernel corn

1 small onion, finely chopped (¼ cup)

1½ cups fat-free cholesterol-free egg product

1 can (12 ounces) evaporated fat-free milk

½ cup plain fat-free yogurt

1 tablespoon mustard

1. Heat oven to 350°. Spray square baking dish, 8 × 8 × 2 inches, with cooking spray.

2. Mix bread cubes, cheese, peas and onion in large bowl. Mix remaining ingredients in separate bowl and pour over bread mixture. Stir to coat. Pour into baking dish.

3. Bake uncovered about 30 minutes or until golden brown and center is set.

1 serving: Calories 295 (Calories from Fat 80); Fat 9g (Saturated 5g); Cholesterol 25mg; Sodium 610mg; Carbohydrate 33g (Dietary Fiber 6g); Protein 26g

Betty's Tip

If you're a fan of pumpernickel or light rye bread, use one of them instead of whole wheat.

MAKE IT A MEAL

Serve sausage patties with this dish, followed by fresh seasonal fruit.

Macaroni and Cheese

4 SERVINGS PREP TIME: **25 MINUTES** START TO FINISH: **55 MINUTES**

2 cups uncooked elbow macaroni (7 ounces)

½ stick butter or margarine (¼ cup)

¼ cup all-purpose flour

½ teaspoon salt

¼ teaspoon pepper

¼ teaspoon ground mustard

¼ teaspoon Worcestershire sauce

2 cups milk

2 cups shredded sharp Cheddar cheese (8 ounces)

*Betty's Tip*_____

For variety, mix up your cheeses! Try Vermont white Cheddar or even a mixture of half sharp Cheddar and half Monterey Jack cheese with jalapeño peppers, in this great-tasting comfort food.

1. Heat oven to 350°.

2. Cook and drain macaroni as directed on package.

3. While pasta is cooking, melt butter in 3-quart saucepan over low heat. Stir in flour, salt, pepper, mustard and Worcestershire sauce. Cook over low heat, stirring constantly, until mixture is smooth and bubbly; remove from heat. Stir in milk. Heat to boiling, stirring constantly. Boil and stir 1 minute; remove from heat. Stir in cheese until melted.

4. Gently stir drained macaroni into cheese sauce. Pour into ungreased 2-quart casserole. Bake uncovered 20 to 25 minutes or until bubbly.

1 serving: Calories 605 (Calories from Fat 305); Fat 34g (Saturated 21g); Cholesterol 100mg; Sodium 790mg; Carbohydrate 51g (Dietary Fiber 2g); Protein 26g

MAKE IT A MEAL

For a quick side salad, cut ripe grape or cherry tomatoes in half and toss in a bowl with olive oil, vinegar, salt and pepper. Add some minced scallions or chives, if you have them.

Fettuccine and Broccoli with Sharp Cheddar Sauce

4 SERVINGS PREP TIME: **5 MINUTES** START TO FINISH: **15 MINUTES**

6 ounces uncooked fettuccine, broken into thirds

2 cups frozen broccoli cuts

1 jar (5 ounces) process sharp cheese spread

¼ cup milk

2 tablespoons ¼-inch strips roasted bell peppers (from 7-ounce jar), drained

Betty's Tip_____

If you don't have roasted bell peppers, use canned pimientos.

1. Cook and drain fettuccine as directed on package, except add broccoli about 2 minutes before fettuccine is done. Set aside.

2. Mix cheese spread and milk in saucepan. Cook over medium heat 1 to 3 minutes, stirring frequently, until smooth. Stir in fettuccine, broccoli and bell peppers until coated.

1 serving: Calories 299 (Calories from Fat 90); Fat 10g (Saturated 4g); Cholesterol 27mg; Sodium 382mg; Carbohydrate 40g (Dietary Fiber 3g); Protein 14g

Mozzarella and Tomato Melts

4 SERVINGS PREP TIME: **5 MINUTES** START TO FINISH: **10 MINUTES**

4 slices Italian bread, each 1 inch thick

8 ounces part-skim mozzarella cheese, sliced

2 medium tomatoes, thinly sliced

Salt and freshly ground pepper

½ cup pesto

Fresh basil leaves, if desired

1. Set oven control to broil. Place bread on rack in broiler pan. Broil with tops about 4 inches from heat until golden brown; turn. Divide cheese among bread slices. Broil just until cheese begins to melt.

2. Arrange tomatoes on cheese. Sprinkle with salt and pepper to taste. Top with pesto. Garnish with basil leaves if desired.

1 sandwich: Calories 317 (Calories from Fat 179); Fat 20g (Saturated 8g); Cholesterol 38mg; Sodium 879mg; Carbohydrate 17g (Dietary Fiber 3g); Protein 18g

Betty's Tip

You'll be craving these melts in the summer when tomatoes are so juicy and ripe. You'll hardly be able to wait the few minutes it takes to make these sandwiches!

MAKE IT A MEAL

Prepare a big antipasto salad with torn romaine leaves, slivers of Genoa salami, sliced cucumbers, and chopped red onion tossed with your favorite Italian dressing.

Fruited Gorgonzola and Cheddar Melts

4 SERVINGS PREP TIME: **5 MINUTES** START TO FINISH: **10 MINUTES**

4 slices whole grain bread, each 1 inch thick

1 large apple, cored and cut into 8 rings

1 large pear, sliced

4 ounces Cheddar cheese, sliced

4 ounces Gorgonzola cheese, crumbled

1. Set oven control to broil. Place bread on ungreased cookie sheet. Broil with tops about 4 inches from heat 1 minute or until golden brown.

2. Turn bread. Divide apple rings and pear slices among bread slices. Top with Cheddar and Gorgonzola cheeses. Broil 2 to 4 minutes or just until cheese begins to melt.

1 sandwich: Calories 349 (Calories from Fat 173); Fat 19g (Saturated 11g); Cholesterol 50mg; Sodium 716mg; Carbohydrate 27g (Dietary Fiber 6g); Protein 17g

Betty's Tip

Toasted walnuts taste terrific with Gorgonzola cheese! Sprinkle toasted or plain walnuts over pear slices before adding cheese.

MAKE IT A MEAL

A soup and sandwich combination is one of the quickest and most satisfying suppers you can make. Split pea soup goes very well with these savory melts. Heat your favorite canned soup or plan ahead by cooking a batch of homemade soup on the weekend. Refrigerate for up to 3 days or freeze for up to 3 months.

Chicken Quesadilla Sandwiches

4 SERVINGS PREP TIME: **15 MINUTES** START TO FINISH: **1 HOUR**

2 teaspoons vegetable oil

1 pound boneless, skinless chicken breasts

¼ cup chopped fresh cilantro

¼ teaspoon ground cumin

8 flour tortillas (8 to 10 inches in diameter)

1 cup shredded Monterey Jack cheese (4 ounces)

1 can (4 ounces) chopped green chilies, drained

Salsa, if desired

SPEED SUPPER

Cut up to 20 minutes of prep time by starting with purchased cooked chicken breast or leftover roast chicken.

1. Heat oil in 10-inch nonstick skillet over medium-high heat. Cook chicken, cilantro and cumin in oil 15 to 20 minutes, turning chicken once and stirring cilantro mixture occasionally, until juice of chicken is no longer pink when centers of thickest pieces are cut. Shred chicken into small pieces. Mix chicken and cilantro mixture. Remove mixture from skillet and wipe out skillet.

2. Spray 1 side of 1 tortilla with cooking spray. Place sprayed side down in same skillet. Layer with one-fourth of the chicken mixture, ¼ cup of the cheese and one-fourth of the chilies to within ½ inch of edge of tortilla. Top with another tortilla and spray top of tortilla with cooking spray.

3. Cook over medium-high heat 4 to 6 minutes, turning after 2 minutes, until light golden brown. Repeat with remaining tortillas, chicken mixture, cheese and chilies. Cut quesadillas into wedges. Serve with salsa if desired.

1 sandwich: Calories 495 (Calories from Fat 180); Fat 20g (Saturated 7g); Cholesterol 75mg; Sodium 690mg; Carbohydrate 50g (Dietary Fiber 3g); Protein 32g

Cheddar-Stuffed Chicken Breasts

4 SERVINGS PREP TIME: **15 MINUTES** START TO FINISH: **30 MINUTES**

4 boneless, skinless chicken breast halves (about 1¼ pounds)

¼ teaspoon salt

¼ teaspoon pepper

3 ounces Cheddar cheese

1 tablespoon butter or margarine, melted

¼ cup salsa

1. Heat coals or gas grill for direct heat. Flatten each chicken breast half to ¼-inch thickness between sheets of plastic wrap or waxed paper. Sprinkle with salt and pepper.

2. Cut cheese into 4 slices, about 3 × 1 × 3¼ inch. Place 1 slice cheese on center of each chicken piece. Roll chicken around cheese, folding in sides. Brush rolls with butter.

3. Cover and grill chicken rolls, seam sides down, 4 to 5 inches from medium heat about 15 minutes, turning after 10 minutes, until juice of chicken is no longer pink in center. Serve with salsa.

1 serving: Calories 250 (Calories from Fat 115); Fat 13g (Saturated 7g); Cholesterol 100mg; Sodium 400mg; Carbohydrate 1g (Dietary Fiber 0g); Protein 32g

MAKE IT A MEAL

Enjoy these chicken rolls with bow-tie noodles tossed with fresh chopped parsley and steamed green beans.

Sausage, Cheese and Tomato Strata

12 SERVINGS PREP TIME: **15 MINUTES** START TO FINISH: **3 HOURS**

1 pound bulk turkey sausage

8 slices 100% whole wheat bread,
  cut into 1-inch cubes (7 cups)

2 cups shredded Gruyère cheese (8 ounces)

6 medium roma (plum) tomatoes, chopped
  (2 cups)

6 eggs

2 cups milk

2 teaspoons dried basil leaves

2 teaspoons Dijon mustard

½ teaspoon salt

Betty's Tip

Sensational on many counts, this strata is a great way to get whole grain—it comes from the bread. It's a super do-ahead breakfast if you assemble the strata the night before and refrigerate, and it's delicious as well as pretty. Family members or guests will ask for more!

1. Cook sausage in 10-inch skillet over medium-high heat 5 to 7 minutes, stirring occasionally, until no longer pink; drain.

2. Spray rectangular baking dish, $13 \times 9 \times 2$ inches, with cooking spray. Spread bread cubes in baking dish. Spread sausage evenly over bread. Sprinkle evenly with 1½ cups of the cheese and the tomatoes.

3. Beat eggs, milk, basil, mustard and salt in medium bowl with fork or wire whisk. Pour over tomatoes. Sprinkle with remaining ½ cup cheese. Cover tightly and refrigerate at least 2 hours but not longer than 24 hours.

4. Heat oven to 350°. Uncover baking dish and bake 35 to 40 minutes or until knife inserted in center comes out clean.

1 serving: Calories 280 (Calories from Fat 130); Fat 15g (Saturated 6g); Cholesterol 165mg; Sodium 610mg; Carbohydrate 14g (Dietary Fiber 2g); Protein 22g

Lox and Cream Cheese Scramble

4 SERVINGS PREP TIME: **10 MINUTES** START TO FINISH: **20 MINUTES**

1 teaspoon canola oil

8 eggs or 16 egg whites

¼ teaspoon dried dill weed

¼ teaspoon salt

2 medium green onions, chopped
(2 tablespoons)

3 ounces salmon lox, chopped

2 tablespoons reduced-fat cream cheese
(Neufchâtel)

Reduced-fat sour cream, if desired

Capers, if desired

1. Coat 12-inch nonstick skillet with oil and heat over medium heat. Beat eggs, dill weed and salt in large bowl with fork or wire whisk until well blended. Pour egg mixture into skillet. Cook uncovered 4 minutes. As mixture begins to set on bottom and side, gently lift cooked portions with spatula so that thin, uncooked portion can flow to bottom. Avoid constant stirring.

2. Gently stir in onions and lox. Drop cream cheese by teaspoonfuls onto mixture. Cook 4 to 5 minutes, stirring gently, until eggs are thickened but still moist. Garnish with sour cream and capers if desired.

1 serving: Calories 200 (Calories from Fat 130); Fat 14g (Saturated 4.5g); Cholesterol 435mg; Sodium 460mg; Carbohydrate 2g (Dietary Fiber 0g); Protein 17g

MAKE IT A MEAL

Serve with toasted English muffins or bagels.

Ham and Herbed Cheese Latkes

4 SERVINGS PREP TIME: **10 MINUTES** START TO FINISH: **20 MINUTES**

2 cups soft bread crumbs (about 3 slices)

1 cup chopped fully cooked ham

4 medium green onions, chopped (¼ cup)

4 eggs, beaten

½ bag (1-pound 4-ounce size) refrigerated shredded hash brown potatoes (1½ cups)

1 container (5 ounces) garlic-and-herb spreadable cheese

1 tablespoon vegetable oil

½ cup sour cream

1. Mix all ingredients except oil and sour cream.

2. Heat oil in 12-inch nonstick skillet over medium heat. Spoon potato mixture into 4 mounds in skillet; flatten slightly. Cook 6 to 8 minutes, turning once, until deep golden brown.

3. Serve with sour cream. Sprinkle with additional chopped green onion if desired.

1 serving: Calories 436 (Calories from Fat 235); Fat 26g (Saturated 13g); Cholesterol 275mg; Sodium 864mg; Carbohydrate 31g (Dietary Fiber 2g); Protein 17g

Betty's Tip

One 2-ounce jar of diced pimientos or 1 small red bell pepper, chopped, would add bright red color to these soft potato pancakes.

MAKE IT A MEAL

Serve with fresh cut-up fruit and your favorite bakery muffins.

Denver Pocket Sandwiches

6 SERVINGS PREP TIME: **10 MINUTES** START TO FINISH: **15 MINUTES**

2 tablespoons margarine or butter

1 medium onion, chopped (½ cup)

1 small green bell pepper, chopped (½ cup)

6 large eggs

½ cup chopped fully cooked smoked ham,
   or 1 can (5 ounces) chunk ham

1 jar (2 ounces) diced pimientos, drained

¼ teaspoon salt

⅛ teaspoon pepper

3 pita breads (6 inches in diameter),
   cut in half to form pockets

1. Melt margarine in 10-inch skillet over medium heat. Cook onion and bell pepper in margarine, stirring occasionally, until onion is tender.

2. Beat eggs slightly in medium bowl. Stir in ham, pimientos, salt and pepper. Pour egg mixture into skillet. Cook over low heat, gently lifting cooked portions with spatula so that thin, uncooked portion can flow to bottom. Avoid constant stirring. Cook 3 to 5 minutes or until eggs are thickened throughout but still moist.

3. Divide egg mixture among pita breads.

1 sandwich: Calories 212 (Calories from Fat 87); Fat 10g (Saturated 2g); Cholesterol 216mg; Sodium 485mg; Carbohydrate 20g (Dietary Fiber 1g); Protein 11g

MAKE IT A MEAL

Bulk up these tasty sandwiches with just a few extra calories and no extra fat, for a super-hearty meal. Line the pita breads with salad greens, alfalfa sprouts, tomato slices, shredded carrot, pea pods or sliced mushrooms before filling with the egg mixture.

CHAPTER 3

Hearty Vegetable and Bean Dinners

Vegetable Kung Pao

4 SERVINGS PREP TIME: **5 MINUTES** START TO FINISH: **15 MINUTES**

½ cup dry-roasted peanuts

Cooking spray

1 tablespoon cornstarch

1 teaspoon sugar

1 tablespoon cold water

½ cup chicken broth

1 teaspoon chili puree with garlic

1 bag (16 ounces) frozen whole baby carrots, green beans and yellow beans

Hot cooked rice, if desired

1. Spray nonstick wok or 12-inch nonstick skillet with cooking spray and heat over medium-high heat. Spread peanuts in single layer on paper towel. Lightly spray with cooking spray, about 2 seconds. Add peanuts to wok and stir-fry about 1 minute or until toasted. Immediately remove from wok; cool.

2. Mix cornstarch, sugar and cold water; set aside. Mix broth and chili puree in wok and heat to boiling. Stir in frozen vegetables. Heat to boiling, then reduce heat to medium-low. Cover and cook 5 minutes, stirring occasionally.

3. Move vegetables to side of wok. Stir cornstarch mixture into liquid in wok. Cook and stir vegetables and sauce over high heat about 1 minute or until sauce is thickened. Stir in peanuts. Serve with rice if desired.

1 serving: Calories 95 (Calories from Fat 35); Fat 4g (Saturated 2g); Cholesterol 0mg; Sodium 190mg; Carbohydrate 11g (Dietary Fiber 3g); Protein 7g

Bok Choy and Cashew Stir-Fry

4 SERVINGS PREP TIME: **12 MINUTES** START TO FINISH: **20 MINUTES**

½ cup vegetable or chicken broth

2 tablespoons soy sauce

4 teaspoons cornstarch

6 stalks bok choy

2 tablespoons vegetable oil

1 large onion, sliced and separated into rings

2 cloves garlic, finely chopped

1 teaspoon finely chopped gingerroot

½ pound mushrooms, cut in halves

½ cup cashews or peanuts

Betty's Tip

Bok choy is a leafy green vegetable that resembles celery in shape but has white stalks and dark green leaves. The leaves are often separated and added after the stalks are cooked, to prevent overcooking.

1. Mix broth, soy sauce and cornstarch; set aside. Separate bok choy leaves from stems. Cut leaves and stems into 1-inch pieces.

2. Heat oil in 12-inch nonstick skillet or wok over medium-high heat. Add bok choy stems, onion, garlic and gingerroot. Cook 2 minutes, stirring constantly. Stir in bok choy leaves and mushrooms. Cook 1 minute, stirring constantly.

3. Stir in cornstarch mixture. Cook, stirring constantly, about 4 minutes or until thickened. Stir in cashews.

1 serving: Calories 201 (Calories from Fat 108); Fat 12g (Saturated 2g); Cholesterol 0mg; Sodium 859mg; Carbohydrate 20g (Dietary Fiber 4g); Protein 9g

MAKE IT A MEAL

For an easy, cooling dessert, toss canned mandarin orange segments (drained) with chopped crystallized ginger and spoon over orange or pineapple sherbet.

Baked Potato Primavera

4 SERVINGS PREP TIME: **5 MINUTES** START TO FINISH: **17 MINUTES**

4 medium unpeeled baking potatoes

½ cup water

1 bag (1 pound) frozen broccoli, carrots and cauliflower

1 container (5 ounces) garlic-and-herb spreadable cheese

Betty's Tip

For variety, try frozen potato patties that are warmed in the toaster.

1. Pierce potatoes to allow steam to escape. Arrange about 1 inch apart in circle on microwavable paper towel in microwave oven. Microwave uncovered on High 8 minutes or until tender.

2. While potatoes are cooking, heat water to boiling in 2-quart saucepan. Stir in vegetables and reduce heat to medium. Cover and simmer 3 to 7 minutes, stirring occasionally, until tender; drain.

3. Stir cheese into vegetables until melted. Cut baked potatoes in half and spoon vegetables over top.

1 serving: Calories 330 (Calories from Fat 89); Fat 10g (Saturated 5g); Cholesterol 24mg; Sodium 282mg; Carbohydrate 51g (Dietary Fiber 6g); Protein 10g

Hot German Potato and Bean Skillet Dinner

4 SERVINGS PREP TIME: **10 MINUTES** START TO FINISH: **20 MINUTES**

2 tablespoons vegetable oil

1 bag (1 pound) frozen green beans, potatoes, onions and red peppers

⅔ cup vegetable or chicken broth

⅓ cup cider vinegar

1 tablespoon sugar

1 tablespoon cornstarch

1 can (15 to 16 ounces) kidney beans, rinsed and drained

1 can (15 to 16 ounces) garbanzo beans, rinsed and drained

2 tablespoons bacon flavor bits or chips, if desired

1. Heat oil in 12-inch nonstick skillet over medium-high heat. Cook vegetables in oil about 5 minutes, stirring frequently, until hot.

2. Mix broth, vinegar, sugar and cornstarch. Stir into vegetables. Heat to boiling. Boil, stirring constantly, until thickened.

3. Stir in beans. Cook until beans are hot. Sprinkle with bacon bits if desired.

1 serving: Calories 301 (Calories from Fat 80); Fat 9g (Saturated 1g); Cholesterol 3mg; Sodium 454mg; Carbohydrate 43g (Dietary Fiber 8g); Protein 11g

Betty's Tip

Vegetarians often substitute arrowroot for cornstarch. Arrowroot, the fine powder from the tropical arrowroot tuber, has no flavor and becomes clear when cooked. Unlike cornstarch, arrowroot doesn't taste chalky when undercooked.

MAKE IT A MEAL

Warm up chunky applesauce in a saucepan on the stove-top or in the microwave. Sprinkle with cinnamon and chopped walnuts.

West African Sweet Potato Supper

6 **SERVINGS** PREP TIME: **15 MINUTES** START TO FINISH: **45 MINUTES**

1 tablespoon vegetable oil

1 medium onion, sliced and separated into rings

¼ cup creamy peanut butter

1 teaspoon chili powder

½ teaspoon ground ginger

½ teaspoon salt

¼ teaspoon ground red pepper (cayenne)

3 large sweet potatoes, peeled and cut into ½-inch cubes (4 cups)

2 cans (14½ ounces each) diced tomatoes with roasted garlic, undrained

1 can (15 to 16 ounces) great northern beans, undrained

1 can (15¼ ounces) whole kernel corn, drained

Hot cooked couscous or rice, if desired

1. Heat oil in 4-quart Dutch oven over medium-high heat. Cook onion in oil, stirring frequently, until tender.

2. Stir in remaining ingredients except couscous. Heat to boiling, then reduce heat to medium-low. Cover and cook about 20 to 25 minutes, stirring occasionally, until potatoes are tender. Serve over couscous if desired.

1 serving: Calories 286 (Calories from Fat 74); Fat 8g (Saturated 1g); Cholesterol 0mg; Sodium 1,082mg; Carbohydrate 44g (Dietary Fiber 9g); Protein 10g

Betty's Tips

To make peeling the sweet potatoes easier, microwave them on High for 2 minutes first.

For a nice color contrast, try a can of black beans instead of the great northern beans.

Savory Potato Supper Cake

6 SERVINGS PREP TIME: **25 MINUTES** START TO FINISH: **1 HOUR 15 MINUTES**

1 cup fat-free ricotta cheese

½ cup soft whole grain or white bread crumbs
(about 1 slice bread)

1 tablespoon chopped fresh or 1 teaspoon
dried marjoram leaves

½ teaspoon salt

¼ teaspoon pepper

⅓ cup fat-free cholesterol-free egg product
or 3 egg whites

4 cups shredded sweet potatoes (1 pound)

4 cups shredded baking potatoes (1 pound)

¾ cup chopped onion

Pear Sauce (right) or 1 cup unsweetened
applesauce

1. Heat oven to 375°. Spray rectangular pan,
13 × 9 × 2 inches, with cooking spray. Mix
cheese, bread crumbs, marjoram, salt,
pepper and egg product in large bowl. Stir in
potatoes and onion. Spread in pan.

2. Bake uncovered 45 to 50 minutes or until
potatoes are tender and golden brown. While
potato mixture is baking, prepare Pear
Sauce. Cut potato mixture into squares.
Serve with sauce.

PEAR SAUCE

3 medium Bosc pears, peeled and chopped
(2 cups)

¼ cup water

2 tablespoons frozen (thawed) apple juice
concentrate

1 teaspoon vanilla

½ teaspoon ground cinnamon

¼ teaspoon ground nutmeg

1. Place all ingredients in 1-quart saucepan and
cook, covered, over medium heat 10 minutes,
stirring occasionally. Reduce heat to
medium-low. Cook about 30 minutes longer,
stirring occasionally, until pears are very
tender.

2. Place mixture in blender or food processor.
Cover and blend until chunky.

1 serving: Calories 215 (Calories from Fat 10); Fat 1g
(Saturated 0g); Cholesterol 0mg; Sodium 340mg;
Carbohydrate 46g (Dietary Fiber 4g); Protein 10g

*Betty's Tip*_____

For a delicious finishing touch, top each
serving with a dollop of reduced-fat sour
cream and a dusting of ground nutmeg.

Mushroom-Pepper Whole Wheat Sandwiches

4 SERVINGS PREP TIME: **14 MINUTES** START TO FINISH: **30 MINUTES**

4 medium fresh portabella mushroom caps (3½ to 4 inches)

4 slices red onion, ½ inch thick

2 tablespoons reduced-fat mayonnaise or salad dressing

2 teaspoons reduced-fat balsamic vinaigrette

8 slices whole wheat bread

4 slices (¾ ounce each) part-skim mozzarella cheese

8 strips (2 × 1 inch) roasted red bell peppers (from 7-ounce jar), patted dry

8 large basil leaves

1. Heat closed medium-size contact grill for 5 minutes.

2. Place mushrooms on grill. Close and cook 4 to 5 minutes or until slightly softened. Remove mushrooms and place onion on grill. Close and cook 4 to 5 minutes or until slightly softened. Remove onion from grill.

3. Mix mayonnaise and vinaigrette in small bowl. Spread over bread slices. Top 4 bread slices with mushrooms, cheese, onion, bell pepper and basil. Top with remaining bread, mayonnaise sides down.

4. Place 2 sandwiches on grill. Close grill and cook 2 to 3 minutes or until sandwiches are golden brown and toasted. Repeat with remaining 2 sandwiches.

1 sandwich: Calories 260 (Calories from Fat 80); Fat 9g (Saturated 3g); Cholesterol 10mg; Sodium 440mg; Carbohydrate 32g (Dietary Fiber 5g); Protein 14g

Italian Grinders

4 SERVINGS PREP TIME: **10 MINUTES** START TO FINISH: **25 MINUTES**

4 frozen vegetable burgers, thawed

3 tablespoons grated Parmesan cheese

1 teaspoon Italian seasoning

4 teaspoons olive or vegetable oil

1 small onion, cut in half and sliced

1 small red bell pepper, cut into ¼-inch strips

1 small green bell pepper, cut into ¼-inch strips

4 hot dog buns, split

½ cup tomato pasta sauce, heated

1. Crumble burgers and mix with cheese and Italian seasoning. Shape mixture into 16 balls. Heat 2 teaspoons of the oil in 10-inch nonstick skillet over medium heat. Cook burger balls in oil, turning frequently, until brown. Remove from skillet; keep warm.

2. Heat remaining 2 teaspoons oil in same skillet over medium heat. Cook onion and bell peppers in oil, stirring frequently, until crisp-tender.

3. Place 4 burger balls in each bun. Top with vegetable mixture. Serve with pasta sauce.

1 sandwich: Calories 349 (Calories from Fat 127); Fat 14g (Saturated 3g); Cholesterol 3mg; Sodium 654mg; Carbohydrate 33g (Dietary Fiber 4g); Protein 22g

MAKE IT A MEAL

Toss bagged shredded carrots with some torn fresh basil and bottled Parmesan salad dressing.

Vegetable Tortillas

6 SERVINGS PREP TIME: **10 MINUTES** START TO FINISH: **28 MINUTES**

1 small red bell pepper, chopped (½ cup)

1 small yellow bell pepper, chopped (½ cup)

½ cup chopped chayote or zucchini

6 fat-free flour tortillas (6 to 8 inches in diameter)

1½ cups shredded reduced-fat Monterey Jack cheese (6 ounces)

Cooking spray

Betty's Tip

Chayote, a fruit that resembles a large pear in size and shape, is an interesting change of pace from the usual zucchini and yellow squash. Chayote are most widely available during the winter months, but you may be able to find them in some supermarkets all year long.

1. Mix bell peppers and chayote. Spoon ¼ cup of the vegetable mixture onto center of each tortilla. Top each with ¼ cup of the cheese. Roll tortilla tightly around vegetable mixture.

2. Spray 10-inch nonstick skillet with cooking spray and heat over medium heat. Cook 2 filled tortillas, seam sides down, in skillet about 3 minutes or until bottoms are light brown. Spray tops of tortillas lightly with cooking spray and turn tortillas. Cook about 3 minutes longer or until bottoms are light brown. Repeat with remaining tortillas.

1 serving: Calories 190 (Calories from Fat 45); Fat 5g (Saturated 3g); Cholesterol 15mg; Sodium 490mg; Carbohydrate 26g (Dietary Fiber 1g); Protein 11g

Minestrone Soup

6 SERVINGS PREP TIME: **15 MINUTES** START TO FINISH: **40 MINUTES**

1 can (28 ounces) whole tomatoes, undrained

1 can (15 to 16 ounces) great northern beans, undrained

1 can (15 to 16 ounces) kidney beans, undrained

1 can (15.25 ounces) whole kernel corn, undrained

2 medium stalks celery, thinly sliced (1 cup)

1 small zucchini, sliced (1 cup)

1 medium onion, chopped (½ cup)

1 cup shredded cabbage

½ cup uncooked elbow macaroni or broken spaghetti

2 cups water

1 teaspoon Italian seasoning

1 extra-large vegetarian vegetable bouillon cube

1 clove garlic, finely chopped

Grated Parmesan cheese, if desired

1. Heat all ingredients except cheese to boiling in 4-quart Dutch oven, breaking up tomatoes. Reduce heat to low.

2. Cover and simmer 15 to 20 minutes, stirring occasionally, until macaroni and vegetables are tender. Serve with cheese if desired.

1 serving: Calories 320 (Calories from Fat 15); Fat 1.5g (Saturated 0g); Cholesterol 0mg; Sodium 860mg; Carbohydrate 59g (Dietary Fiber 12g); Protein 16g

Betty's Tip

For a heartier minestrone, start with 1 pound ground beef. Cook, stirring occasionally, until beef is brown; drain. Add to the ingredients in step 1. Continue with step 2.

MAKE IT A MEAL

For a quick pizza sandwich, toast bread or English muffins and top with pizza sauce, cheese and your favorite toppings. Broil until cheese is melted.

Sweet-and-Sour Oriental Pasta Salad

6 SERVINGS PREP TIME: **10 MINUTES** START TO FINISH: **20 MINUTES**

3 ounces uncooked capellini (angel hair) pasta, broken in half

4 cups shredded Chinese (napa) cabbage

1 cup sliced mushrooms (3 ounces)

1 cup snow (Chinese) pea pods, cut in half (4 ounces)

1 can (8 ounces) sliced water chestnuts, drained

¾ cup sweet-and-sour sauce

⅓ cup plain yogurt

½ cup chopped salted cashews

1. Cook and drain pasta as directed on package. Rinse with cold water; drain.

2. Place pasta, cabbage, mushrooms, pea pods and water chestnuts in large bowl. Mix sweet-and-sour sauce and yogurt with fork. Pour over salad and toss until coated. Sprinkle with cashews.

1 serving: Calories 198 (Calories from Fat 67); Fat 8g (Saturated 2g); Cholesterol 1mg; Sodium 206mg; Carbohydrate 27g (Dietary Fiber 4g); Protein 7g

Betty's Tip

Cashews are the nut of the cashew apple. Their high fat content gives them their delicious buttery flavor. Because of that fat, cashews should be stored in the refrigerator or freezer so they don't become rancid.

Butter Bean Patties with Southwestern Sauce

4 SERVINGS PREP TIME: **12 MINUTES** START TO FINISH: **30 MINUTES**

1 can (15 to 16 ounces) butter beans, rinsed and drained

10 round buttery crackers, crushed (⅓ cup)

1 egg, beaten

2 tablespoons chili sauce

2 tablespoons finely chopped onion

Southwestern Sauce (right)

1. Mash beans in medium bowl. Stir in crackers, egg, chili sauce and onion. Shape mixture into 4 patties, each about ½ inch thick.

2. Spray 10-inch skillet with cooking spray. Cook patties in skillet 8 to 10 minutes, turning once, until golden brown. Remove from skillet; keep warm.

3. Add all Southwestern Sauce ingredients to skillet. Cook over medium-low heat 5 to 8 minutes, stirring occasionally, until vegetables are tender. Serve sauce over patties.

SOUTHWESTERN SAUCE

1 cup frozen mixed vegetables

¼ cup raisins

¼ teaspoon ground cumin

1 can (14½ ounces) Mexican-style stewed tomatoes with jalapeños and spices, undrained

1 serving: Calories 208 (Calories from Fat 40); Fat 4g (Saturated 1g); Cholesterol 106mg; Sodium 936mg; Carbohydrate 38g (Dietary Fiber 6g); Protein 9g

Betty's Tip

If you don't have chili sauce or cumin, use ketchup and dried oregano leaves instead.

MAKE IT A MEAL

For a Southwestern cheeseburger, top each patty with a slice of American cheese after turning and serve in a hamburger bun topped with Southwestern Sauce.

Italian Barley and Bean Pilaf

6 SERVINGS PREP TIME: **8 MINUTES** START TO FINISH: **30 MINUTES**

2 tablespoons garlic-flavored oil

1 large onion, chopped (1 cup)

6 ounces portabella mushrooms, sliced

2 cans (14½ ounces each) diced tomatoes with basil, garlic and oregano, undrained

¾ cup uncooked quick-cooking barley

1 teaspoon dried thyme leaves

1 can (15 to 19 ounces) cannellini beans, rinsed and drained

3 cups lightly packed washed fresh spinach leaves, cut into ½-inch strips

¾ cup shredded Parmesan cheese

1. Heat oil in 12-inch nonstick skillet over medium-high heat. Cook onion and mushrooms in oil, stirring frequently, until tender.

2. Stir in tomatoes, barley and thyme; reduce heat to low. Cover and simmer 12 to 15 minutes, stirring occasionally, until barley is tender.

3. Stir in beans, spinach and ½ cup of the cheese. Cook until hot. Sprinkle with remaining ¼ cup cheese.

1 serving: Calories 264 (Calories from Fat 71); Fat 8g (Saturated 2g); Cholesterol 7mg; Sodium 626mg; Carbohydrate 36g (Dietary Fiber 9g); Protein 11g

Betty's Tips

Regular white mushrooms, cut in half, can be used in place of the portabella mushrooms in this hearty and robust Italian skillet dish.

Use regular vegetable or olive oil and half a teaspoon of garlic powder in place of the flavored oil.

MAKE IT A MEAL

For a quick salad, mix marinated artichokes (with marinade), olives and torn greens with leftover cooked vegetables such as broccoli.

Savory Black-Eyed Peas

4 SERVINGS PREP TIME: **5 MINUTES** START TO FINISH: **20 MINUTES**

1 cup chicken broth

3 medium carrots, thinly sliced (1½ cups)

2 medium stalks celery, sliced (1 cup)

1 large onion, chopped (1 cup)

1½ tablespoons chopped fresh or 1½ teaspoons dried savory or basil leaves

1 clove garlic, finely chopped

1 can (15 to 16 ounces) black-eyed peas, rinsed and drained

½ cup shredded reduced-fat Monterey Jack cheese (2 ounces)

1. Heat broth, carrots, celery, onion, savory and garlic to boiling in 10-inch nonstick skillet. Reduce heat to medium. Cook 8 to 10 minutes, stirring occasionally, until vegetables are tender.

2. Stir in black-eyed peas. Cook, stirring occasionally, until hot. Sprinkle with cheese.

1 serving: Calories 160 (Calories from Fat 25); Fat 3g (Saturated 2g); Cholesterol 10mg; Sodium 440mg; Carbohydrate 29g (Dietary Fiber 8g); Protein 12g

*Betty's Tip*_____

The mild, peppery flavor of fresh savory is a cross between mint and thyme.

MAKE IT A MEAL

Serve the stew over a bed of seasoned instant couscous.

Black-Eyed Pea and Sausage Soup

6 SERVINGS PREP TIME: **15 MINUTES** START TO FINISH: **9 HOURS 30 MINUTES**

2 cans (15 to 16 ounces each) black-eyed peas, rinsed and drained

12 ounces smoked turkey kielbasa (Polish sausage), cut lengthwise in half, then sliced crosswise

4 medium carrots, chopped (2 cups)

4 cloves garlic, finely chopped

1 cup uncooked wheat berries

2 cups water

3 cans (14 ounces each) reduced-sodium beef broth

2 cups shredded washed fresh spinach

1 teaspoon dried marjoram leaves

1. Mix all ingredients except spinach and marjoram in 3- to 4-quart slow cooker.

2. Cover and cook on low heat setting 8 to 9 hours.

3. Stir in spinach and marjoram. Cover and cook on low heat setting about 15 minutes longer or until spinach is tender.

1 serving: Calories 350 (Calories from Fat 70); Fat 8g (Saturated 2g); Cholesterol 30mg; Sodium 950mg; Carbohydrate 47g (Dietary Fiber 9g); Protein 25g

Betty's Tips

Offer diners Dijon mustard and horseradish to stir into this Southern-style soup. Try other greens, such as Swiss chard, mustard greens or turnip greens, solo or in combination with the spinach. You might also try andouille sausage, a Cajun favorite, to give this soup a kick.

MAKE IT A MEAL

Whip up a batch of corn muffins from your favorite recipe or a mix and serve piping hot.

Indian Lentils and Rice

6 SERVINGS PREP TIME: **15 MINUTES** START TO FINISH: **55 MINUTES**

4 medium green onions, chopped (¼ cup)

1 tablespoon finely chopped gingerroot

⅛ teaspoon crushed red pepper

2 cloves garlic, finely chopped

1 can (49½ ounces) or 3 cans (14½ ounces each) vegetable broth

1½ cups dried lentils (12 ounces), sorted and rinsed

1 teaspoon ground turmeric

½ teaspoon salt

1 large tomato, chopped (1 cup)

¼ cup shredded coconut

2 tablespoons chopped fresh or 2 teaspoons dried mint leaves

3 cups hot cooked rice

1½ cups plain fat-free yogurt

1. Spray 3-quart saucepan with cooking spray. Cook onions, gingerroot, red pepper and garlic in saucepan over medium heat 3 to 5 minutes, stirring occasionally, until onions are tender.

2. Stir in 5 cups of the broth, the lentils, turmeric and salt. Heat to boiling; reduce heat. Cover and simmer 25 to 30 minutes, adding remaining broth if needed, until lentils are tender. Stir in tomato, coconut and mint. Serve over rice with yogurt.

1 serving: Calories 290 (Calories from Fat 20); Fat 2g (Saturated 1g); Cholesterol 0mg; Sodium 1,120mg; Carbohydrate 61g (Dietary Fiber 11g); Protein 18g

MAKE IT A MEAL
Creamy Dilled Cucumbers

6 SERVINGS PREP TIME: **10 MINUTES** START TO FINISH: **4 HOURS 10 MINUTES**

½ cup plain fat-free yogurt

1 teaspoon chopped fresh or ¼ teaspoon dried dill weed

½ teaspoon salt

⅛ teaspoon pepper

2 small cucumbers, sliced (2 cups)

1 small red onion, thinly sliced and separated into rings

Mix all ingredients. Cover and refrigerate at least 4 hours to blend flavors.

1 serving: Calories 25 (Calories from Fat 0); Fat 0g (Saturated 0g); Cholesterol 0mg; Sodium 210mg; Carbohydrate 4g (Dietary Fiber 0g); Protein 2g

SPEED SUPPER
Prepare the cucumbers the night before and refrigerate in an airtight container.

Cuban Black Beans and Rice

6 SERVINGS PREP TIME: **15 MINUTES** START TO FINISH: **1 HOUR 5 MINUTES**

1 large onion, chopped (1 cup)

1 medium green bell pepper, chopped (1 cup)

2 medium carrots, chopped (1 cup)

1 cup orange juice

2 teaspoons paprika

1 teaspoon ground coriander

⅛ teaspoon crushed red pepper

1 can (14½ ounces) whole tomatoes, undrained

2 cloves garlic, finely chopped

1 can (15 ounces) black beans, rinsed and drained

4 cups hot cooked brown rice

1 cup plain fat-free yogurt

Paprika, if desired

1 lime, cut into wedges

1. Heat onion, bell pepper, carrots, orange juice, paprika, coriander, red pepper, tomatoes and garlic to boiling in 2-quart saucepan; reduce heat. Cover and simmer about 45 minutes, stirring occasionally, until thickened. Remove from heat and stir in beans.

2. Place 1 cup of the bean mixture in blender or food processor. Cover and blend on medium speed about 30 seconds or until smooth. Stir blended mixture into bean mixture in saucepan. Cook over medium heat about 3 minutes or until hot. Serve over rice with yogurt. Sprinkle with paprika if desired. Serve with lime wedges.

1 serving: Calories 280 (Calories from Fat 20); Fat 2g (Saturated 1g); Cholesterol 0mg; Sodium 150mg; Carbohydrate 61g (Dietary Fiber 8g); Protein 12g

Bean and Cheese Burritos

4 SERVINGS PREP TIME: **10 MINUTES** START TO FINISH: **20 MINUTES**

8 fat-free flour tortillas (6 to 8 inches in diameter)

⅓ cup finely chopped onion

⅓ cup finely chopped green bell pepper

1 can (16 ounces) fat-free refried beans

1¼ cups taco sauce

1 cup shredded reduced-fat Cheddar cheese (4 ounces)

Choice of toppings, if desired (shredded lettuce, chopped tomatoes, chopped ripe olives, plain low-fat or fat-free yogurt and/or reduced-fat sour cream)

Betty's Tips

Sprinkle chopped fresh cilantro or parsley over these burritos for a splash of color and a fresh taste. For a bold flavor, use sharp reduced-fat Cheddar cheese instead of mild. For a more subtle flavor, substitute part-skim mozzarella cheese for the Cheddar.

1. Heat tortillas as directed on package. While tortillas are heating, spray 10-inch nonstick skillet with cooking spray and heat over medium heat. Cook onion and bell pepper in skillet about 5 minutes, stirring frequently, until vegetables are tender. Stir in refried beans and ¼ cup of the taco sauce; heat through.

2. Heat remaining 1 cup taco sauce in 1-quart saucepan over medium heat about 2 minutes, stirring occasionally, until heated through. Remove from heat and cover to keep warm.

3. Place about ⅓ cup of bean mixture on center of each tortilla. Fold one end of tortilla up about 1 inch over filling. Fold right and left sides over folded end, overlapping. Fold remaining end down.

4. Spoon warm taco sauce over burritos. Sprinkle with cheese. Serve with choice of toppings if desired.

1 serving: Calories 255 (Calories from Fat 25); Fat 3g (Saturated 1g); Cholesterol 5mg; Sodium 1,160mg; Carbohydrate 49g (Dietary Fiber 9g); Protein 17g

Black Bean Tacos

4 SERVINGS PREP TIME: **15 MINUTES** START TO FINISH: **30 MINUTES**

2 cans (15 ounces each) black beans, rinsed and drained

1 medium onion, chopped (½ cup)

1 small green bell pepper, chopped (½ cup)

2 cloves garlic, finely chopped

1 jar (8 ounces) taco sauce or salsa (1 cup)

8 taco shells

½ cup shredded lettuce

1 small tomato, chopped (½ cup)

½ cup reduced-fat sour cream

Betty's Tip

In a pinch, make these tacos with canned pinto or red beans instead of the black beans.

1. Mash beans from 1 can of beans; set aside.

2. Spray 10-inch nonstick skillet with cooking spray and heat over medium heat. Cook onion, bell pepper and garlic in skillet about 5 minutes, stirring frequently, until vegetables are tender.

3. Stir in mashed beans, remaining beans and the taco sauce. Heat to boiling; reduce heat. Simmer uncovered 5 minutes.

4. Spoon about ¼ cup bean mixture into each taco shell. Top with lettuce, tomato and sour cream.

1 serving: Calories 455 (Calories from Fat 90); Fat 10g (Saturated 3g); Cholesterol 10mg; Sodium 1,100mg; Carbohydrate 85g (Dietary Fiber 18g); Protein 24g

Ratatouille Chili

4 SERVINGS PREP TIME: **15 MINUTES** START TO FINISH: **35 MINUTES**

2 tablespoons olive or vegetable oil

1 large eggplant (1 pound), cut into ½-inch cubes (4 cups)

1 large onion, chopped (1 cup)

1 medium green bell pepper, chopped (1 cup)

1 clove garlic, finely chopped

½ cup sliced zucchini

3 teaspoons chili powder

1 teaspoon chopped fresh or ¼ teaspoon dried basil leaves

¼ teaspoon salt

1 can (15 to 16 ounces) great northern beans, rinsed and drained

1 can (14½ ounces) whole tomatoes, undrained

1 can (8 ounces) tomato sauce

1. Heat oil in 4-quart Dutch oven over medium-high heat. Cook eggplant, onion, bell pepper and garlic in oil, stirring occasionally, until vegetables are crisp-tender.

2. Stir in remaining ingredients, breaking up tomatoes. Cook about 10 minutes, stirring occasionally, until zucchini is tender.

1 serving: Calories 199 (Calories from Fat 66); Fat 7g (Saturated 1g); Cholesterol 0mg; Sodium 898mg; Carbohydrate 33g (Dietary Fiber 13g); Protein 8g

Betty's Tip

From the Provence region of France, the popular dish of ratatouille includes eggplant, zucchini, tomatoes, olive oil and garlic, all of which are found in this savory chili version.

MAKE IT A MEAL

Accompany with warm French bread.

Cheesy Double-Bean Chili

6 SERVINGS PREP TIME: **15 MINUTES** START TO FINISH: **35 MINUTES**

2 tablespoons margarine or butter

1 medium onion, sliced

1 large clove garlic, finely chopped

1 can (28 ounces) whole tomatoes, undrained

1 can (15 to 16 ounces) kidney beans, rinsed and drained

1 can (15 to 16 ounces) pinto beans, rinsed and drained

1 can (4 ounces) chopped green chilies, drained

2 to 3 teaspoons chipotle chili powder or regular chili powder

½ cup shredded Cheddar cheese (2 ounces)

1 cup shredded Monterey Jack cheese (4 ounces)

1. Melt margarine in 3-quart saucepan over medium heat. Cook onion and garlic in margarine, stirring occasionally, until onion is tender.

2. Stir in remaining ingredients except cheeses, breaking up tomatoes. Heat to boiling; reduce heat. Cover and simmer 15 minutes, stirring occasionally.

3. Stir in Cheddar cheese and ½ cup of the Monterey Jack cheese. Heat over low heat, stirring occasionally, just until cheeses are melted. Sprinkle each serving with remaining Monterey Jack cheese.

1 serving: Calories 277 (Calories from Fat 121); Fat 13g (Saturated 6g); Cholesterol 27mg; Sodium 609mg; Carbohydrate 26g (Dietary Fiber 9g); Protein 14g

Betty's Tip

Chipotle chili powder adds a complex, deep, smoky flavor in this chili. Chipotle chili powder comes from ground chipotle chilies, which are dried, smoked jalapeño chilies.

MAKE IT A MEAL

Combine fresh diced pineapple with some sliced strawberries. Add vanilla yogurt to taste and toss gently.

Hearty Bean and Pasta Stew

4 SERVINGS PREP TIME: **10 MINUTES** START TO FINISH: **30 MINUTES**

1 cup uncooked medium pasta shells (3½ ounces)

¼ cup chopped green bell pepper

1 tablespoon chopped fresh or 1 teaspoon dried basil leaves

1 teaspoon Worcestershire sauce

1 clove garlic, finely chopped

1 large tomato, coarsely chopped (1 cup)

1 small onion, chopped (¼ cup)

1 can (15 to 16 ounces) kidney beans, drained

½ can (15- to 16-ounce size) garbanzo beans, drained

1 can (14½ ounces) vegetable broth

1. Mix all ingredients in 2-quart saucepan. Heat to boiling, stirring occasionally, then reduce heat.

2. Cover and simmer about 15 minutes, stirring occasionally, until macaroni is tender.

1 serving: Calories 265 (Calories from Fat 20); Fat 2g (Saturated 0g); Cholesterol 0mg; Sodium 730mg; Carbohydrate 57g (Dietary Fiber 11g); Protein 16g

MAKE IT A MEAL
Crunchy Jicama and Melon Salad

6 SERVINGS PREP TIME: **15 MINUTES** START TO FINISH: **2 HOURS 15 MINUTES**

1½ cups julienne strips jicama (½ medium)

1½ cups ½-inch cubes cantaloupe (½ medium)

1 teaspoon grated lime peel

3 tablespoons lime juice

2 tablespoons chopped fresh or 1 tablespoon dried mint leaves

1 teaspoon honey

¼ teaspoon salt

Mix all ingredients in glass or plastic bowl. Cover and refrigerate about 2 hours or until chilled.

1 serving: Calories 30 (Calories from Fat 0); Fat 0g (Saturated 0g); Cholesterol 0mg; Sodium 105mg; Carbohydrate 8g (Dietary Fiber 2g); Protein 1g

Betty's Tip

Get to know jicama! It may look ugly on the outside, but it's terrific on the inside. Jicama stays crisp and crunchy and tastes somewhat like water chestnuts, only moister and sweeter.

Mixed-Bean Stew
with Cottage Dumplings

6 SERVINGS PREP TIME: **15 MINUTES** START TO FINISH: **40 MINUTES**

Cottage Dumplings (right)

1 can (15 to 16 ounces) great northern, cannellini or navy beans, rinsed and drained

1 can (15 ounces) black beans, rinsed and drained

1 can (15 ounces) tomato sauce

1 medium red bell pepper, chopped (1 cup)

2 cloves garlic, finely chopped

2 tablespoons chopped fresh or 2 teaspoons dried basil leaves

2 teaspoons olive or vegetable oil

¼ teaspoon pepper

1. Prepare Cottage Dumplings.

2. Heat remaining ingredients to boiling in 3-quart saucepan; reduce heat.

3. Shape dumpling mixture into 12 balls, using about 2 tablespoons each. Carefully slide dumplings onto beans in simmering stew (do not drop directly into liquid). Cook uncovered 10 minutes. Cover and cook about 10 minutes longer or until dumplings are firm.

COTTAGE DUMPLINGS

1 cup shredded reduced-fat Monterey Jack cheese (4 ounces)

⅔ cup frozen (and thawed) or canned (and drained) whole kernel corn

½ cup fat-free small curd cottage cheese

⅓ cup soft whole grain or white bread crumbs

⅓ cup yellow cornmeal

¼ cup fat-free cholesterol-free egg product or 2 egg whites

Mix all ingredients.

1 serving: Calories 350 (Calories from Fat 55); Fat 6g (Saturated 3g); Cholesterol 10mg; Sodium 720mg; Carbohydrate 60g (Dietary Fiber 10g); Protein 24g

SPEED SUPPER
The ingredients for the Mixed-Bean Stew may be combined and refrigerated for up to 24 hours before cooking.

Bean-Pasta Stew

4 SERVINGS PREP TIME: **10 MINUTES** START TO FINISH: **30 MINUTES**

2 cans (15 to 16 ounces each) pinto or navy beans, rinsed and drained

1 can (14½ ounces) Italian-style stewed tomatoes, undrained

1 can (14½ ounces) chicken broth

1 package (10 ounces) frozen cut green beans, thawed

2 medium stalks celery, sliced (1 cup)

1½ teaspoons Italian seasoning

½ cup uncooked small pasta shells or elbow macaroni (2 ounces)

Grated Parmesan cheese, if desired

1. Heat all ingredients except pasta and cheese to boiling in 3-quart saucepan. Reduce heat to low.

2. Stir in pasta. Cover and simmer about 15 minutes, stirring occasionally, until pasta is tender. Serve with cheese if desired.

1 serving: Calories 350 (Calories from Fat 20); Fat 2g (Saturated 1g); Cholesterol 0mg; Sodium 1,130mg; Carbohydrate 81g (Dietary Fiber 22g); Protein 24g

Betty's Tip

Anything goes when it comes to choosing the beans in this stew. You can use the pinto or navy beans suggested, or try lima, cannellini, garbanzo, butter or kidney beans. If you like, use a can each of two different kinds.

Slow-Cooker Lentil Stew with Corn Bread Dumplings

8 SERVINGS PREP TIME: **15 MINUTES** START TO FINISH: **8 HOURS 50 MINUTES**

STEW

- 2 cups dried lentils (1 pound), sorted and rinsed
- 3 cups water
- 1 teaspoon ground cumin
- 1 teaspoon salt-free seasoning blend
- 3 medium carrots, thinly sliced (1½ cups)
- 1 medium yellow or red bell pepper, cut into 1-inch pieces
- 1 medium onion, chopped (½ cup)
- 1 can (14½ ounces) diced tomatoes and green chilies, undrained
- 1 can (14 ounces) vegetable broth

DUMPLINGS

- ½ cup all-purpose flour
- ½ cup yellow cornmeal
- 1 teaspoon baking powder
- ¼ teaspoon salt
- ¼ cup fat-free (skim) milk
- 2 tablespoons canola oil
- 1 egg or 2 egg whites, slightly beaten

1. Mix all stew ingredients in 3½- to 4-quart slow cooker. Cover and cook on low heat setting 7 to 8 hours.

2. Mix flour, cornmeal, baking powder and salt in medium bowl. Stir in milk, oil and egg just until moistened.

3. Drop dough by spoonfuls onto cooked lentil stew. Increase heat setting to high. Cover and cook 25 to 35 minutes or until toothpick inserted in center of dumplings comes out clean.

1 serving: Calories 330 (Calories from Fat 45); Fat 5g (Saturated 0.5g); Cholesterol 25mg; Sodium 650mg; Carbohydrate 52g (Dietary Fiber 12g); Protein 18g

MAKE IT A MEAL

On the side, toss a baby spinach salad with thinly sliced red onion and bottled Italian dressing.

Lentil Stew

2 teaspoons vegetable oil

1 large onion, chopped (1 cup)

1 clove garlic, finely chopped

1 cup dried lentils (8 ounces), sorted and rinsed

¼ cup chopped fresh parsley

3 cups water

½ teaspoon ground cumin

½ teaspoon salt

¼ teaspoon pepper

¼ teaspoon ground mace

2 medium baking potatoes, coarsely chopped

1 package (8 ounces) small white mushrooms, cut in half

1 can (28 ounces) whole tomatoes, undrained

1. Heat oil in Dutch oven over medium-high heat. Cook onion and garlic in oil, stirring frequently, until onion is tender.

2. Stir in remaining ingredients, breaking up tomatoes. Heat to boiling; reduce heat. Cover and simmer about 40 minutes, stirring occasionally, until potatoes are tender.

1 serving: Calories 160 (Calories from Fat 20); Fat 2g (Saturated 0g); Cholesterol 0mg; Sodium 400mg; Carbohydrate 35g (Dietary Fiber 10g); Protein 11g

MAKE IT A MEAL
Honey-Glazed Carrots

6 SERVINGS PREP TIME: 5 MINUTES START TO FINISH: 15 MINUTES

1 bag (16 ounces) baby carrots

2 tablespoons honey

1 tablespoon margarine

Ground nutmeg

1. Place carrots in 1 inch water in 2-quart saucepan. Heat to boiling; reduce heat. Cover and simmer 10 to 15 minutes or until tender. Drain well.

2. Add honey and margarine to carrots in saucepan; heat to boiling. Cook carrots, stirring frequently, until margarine is melted and carrots are glazed. Sprinkle with nutmeg.

1 serving: Calories 70 (Calories from Fat 20); Fat 2g (Saturated 0g); Cholesterol 0mg; Sodium 50mg; Carbohydrate 14g (Dietary Fiber 2g); Protein 1g

Three-Bean and Barley Soup

5 SERVINGS PREP TIME: 10 MINUTES START TO FINISH: 28 MINUTES

1 tablespoon olive or vegetable oil

2 small onions, cut in half and thinly sliced

2 cloves garlic, finely chopped

1 teaspoon ground cumin

1 can (15 to 16 ounces) garbanzo beans, undrained

1 can (15 to 16 ounces) lima beans, drained

1 can (15 ounces) black beans, rinsed and drained

1 can (14½ ounces) Italian-style stewed tomatoes, undrained

½ cup uncooked quick-cooking barley

½ teaspoon salt

3 cups water

2 tablespoons chopped fresh parsley

1. Heat oil in Dutch oven over medium-high heat. Cook onions, garlic and cumin in oil 4 to 5 minutes, stirring occasionally, until onions are tender.

2. Stir in remaining ingredients except parsley. Heat to boiling; reduce heat. Cover and simmer about 10 minutes or until lima beans are tender. Stir in parsley.

1 serving: Calories 370 (Calories from Fat 55); Fat 6g (Saturated 1g); Cholesterol 0mg; Sodium 970mg; Carbohydrate 77g (Dietary Fiber 19g); Protein 21g

Betty's Tip

Mixing grains, such as barley, with beans builds complete proteins. Grains or beans alone don't contain all the protein building blocks our bodies need. But when they are added together, we get all the benefits!

Corn and Black Bean Salad with Tortilla Wedges

4 SERVINGS PREP TIME: **15 MINUTES** START TO FINISH: **20 MINUTES**

4 low-fat flour tortillas (8 to 10 inches in diameter)

2 teaspoons margarine or butter, softened

1 can (15 to 16 ounces) whole kernel corn, drained

1 can (15 ounces) black beans, rinsed and drained

1 medium red bell pepper, chopped (1 cup)

1 small jicama, peeled and diced (2 cups)

½ cup fat-free Italian dressing

½ teaspoon salt

¼ teaspoon pepper

Red leaf lettuce

¼ cup pine nuts, toasted

1. Heat oven to 400°. Spread tortillas with margarine and cut into fourths. Place on ungreased cookie sheet. Bake 4 to 5 minutes or until golden brown.

2. Toss remaining ingredients except lettuce and nuts until mixture is coated with dressing.

3. Serve salad on leaf lettuce. Sprinkle with nuts. Serve with tortilla wedges.

1 serving: Calories 408 (Calories from Fat 113); Fat 13g (Saturated 2g); Cholesterol 1mg; Sodium 1,460mg; Carbohydrate 64g (Dietary Fiber 13g); Protein 12g

Betty's Tips

To toast nuts, bake uncovered in ungreased shallow pan in 350° oven about 10 minutes, stirring occasionally, until golden brown. Or cook in ungreased heavy skillet over medium-low heat 5 to 7 minutes, stirring frequently until browning begins, then stirring constantly until golden brown.

Whole wheat tortillas also make tasty wedges to serve with this salad.

Northern Italian White Bean Salad

6 SERVINGS PREP TIME: **15 MINUTES** START TO FINISH: **2 HOURS 15 MINUTES**

1 large tomato, seeded and coarsely chopped (1 cup)

1 small red bell pepper, chopped (½ cup)

½ cup chopped red onion

¼ cup chopped fresh parsley

¼ cup olive or vegetable oil

2 tablespoons chopped fresh or 2 teaspoons dried basil leaves

2 tablespoons red wine vinegar

½ teaspoon salt

⅛ teaspoon pepper

2 cans (19 ounces each) cannellini beans, rinsed and drained

12 leaves red leaf lettuce

Gently mix all ingredients except lettuce in glass or plastic bowl. Cover and refrigerate at least 2 hours to blend flavors. Serve on lettuce.

1 serving: Calories 245 (Calories from Fat 90); Fat 10g (Saturated 2g); Cholesterol 0mg; Sodium 210mg; Carbohydrate 35g (Dietary Fiber 9g); Protein 13g

SPEED SUPPER
This recipe is adaptable to your schedule. The salad can marinate for as little as 30 minutes or as long as 12 hours.

CHAPTER 4

Delightful Seafood Suppers

Cajun Catfish Sandwiches

4 SERVINGS PREP TIME: **15 MINUTES** START TO FINISH: **40 MINUTES**

1 cup cornflake crumbs

1 tablespoon Cajun or Creole seasoning

¼ cup fat-free (skim) milk

4 catfish fillets (4 ounces each)

1½ cups coleslaw mix (4 ounces)

3 tablespoons fat-free coleslaw dressing

4 whole grain hamburger buns

1 lemon, cut into 4 wedges

1. Heat oven to 425°. Line cookie sheet with foil. Spray with cooking spray.

2. Mix cornflake crumbs and Cajun seasoning in a shallow dish. Pour milk in another shallow dish. Dip each catfish fillet into milk, then coat with cornflake mixture. Place on foil.

3. Bake 10 minutes; turn. Bake 10 to 15 minutes longer or until fish flakes easily with fork.

4. Meanwhile, mix coleslaw mix and dressing in small bowl. Place catfish in buns. Squeeze lemon juice over catfish. Top each fillet with about ¼ cup coleslaw.

1 sandwich: Calories 340 (Calories from Fat 80); Fat 9g (Saturated 2g); Cholesterol 90mg; Sodium 870mg; Carbohydrate 35g (Dietary Fiber 4g); Protein 29g

MAKE IT A MEAL

Double the amount of coleslaw and serve the extra on the side. End the meal with fresh fruit.

Spicy Cornmeal Cod

6 SERVINGS PREP TIME: **10 MINUTES** START TO FINISH: **22 MINUTES**

1½ pounds cod, perch or other lean fish fillets, about ½ inch thick

¾ cup cornmeal

¼ cup all-purpose flour

½ teaspoon salt

½ teaspoon garlic powder

½ teaspoon dried oregano leaves

½ teaspoon ground red pepper (cayenne)

½ teaspoon pepper

2 large eggs, beaten

3 tablespoons margarine or butter, melted

1. Heat oven to 500°.

2. Cut fish fillets into 4 × 2-inch pieces. Mix cornmeal, flour, salt, garlic powder, oregano, red pepper and pepper. Dip fish into eggs, then coat with cornmeal mixture.

3. Place fish on ungreased cookie sheet. Drizzle margarine over fish. Bake 10 to 12 minutes, turning once, until golden brown.

1 serving: Calories 262 (Calories from Fat 73); Fat 8g (Saturated 2g); Cholesterol 119mg; Sodium 345mg; Carbohydrate 21g (Dietary Fiber 1g); Protein 24g

Betty's Tip

Turning the fish over halfway through the baking time helps keep it crispy on both sides.

MAKE IT A MEAL
Hot and Spicy Greens

6 SERVINGS PREP TIME: **5 MINUTES** START TO FINISH: **10 MINUTES**

2 tablespoons margarine or butter

2 pounds collard greens or fresh spinach leaves, washed and coarsely chopped

1 serrano chili, seeded and finely chopped

2 tablespoons finely chopped onion

1 to 2 teaspoons grated gingerroot

1. Melt margarine in Dutch oven over medium heat.

2. Cook remaining ingredients in margarine, stirring frequently, until greens and onion are tender; drain.

1 serving: Calories 81 (Calories from Fat 40); Fat 4g (Saturated 1g); Cholesterol 0mg; Sodium 75mg; Carbohydrate 9g (Dietary Fiber 6g); Protein 4g

Lemon-Pepper Fish Fillet Sandwiches

4 SERVINGS PREP TIME: **11 MINUTES** START TO FINISH: **15 MINUTES**

2 tablespoons yellow cornmeal

2 tablespoons all-purpose flour

1 teaspoon seasoned salt

½ teaspoon lemon-pepper seasoning

1 tablespoon canola oil

2 walleye fillets (about 6 ounces each), each cut crosswise in half

¼ cup tartar sauce

4 100% whole wheat or rye sandwich buns, toasted

1 cup shredded lettuce

1. Mix cornmeal, flour, seasoned salt and lemon-pepper in shallow bowl.

2. Heat oil in 12-inch nonstick skillet over medium-high heat. Coat fish fillets with flour mixture. Cook in oil 4 to 6 minutes, turning once, until fish flakes easily with fork.

3. Spread tartar sauce on cut sides of toasted buns. Layer lettuce and fish fillets in buns.

1 sandwich: Calories 330 (Calories from Fat 130); Fat 14g (Saturated 2g); Cholesterol 50mg; Sodium 930mg; Carbohydrate 29g (Dietary Fiber 2g); Protein 21g

Betty's Tip

Why not try a different type of fish instead of walleye? Tilapia is another mild white fish that is delicious in this recipe.

Flounder with Mushrooms and Wine

4 SERVINGS PREP TIME: **10 MINUTES** START TO FINISH: **30 MINUTES**

1 pound flounder, sole or other delicate fish fillets, about ¾ inch thick

½ teaspoon paprika

½ teaspoon salt

⅛ teaspoon pepper

1 tablespoon margarine or butter

½ cup sliced mushrooms

⅓ cup sliced leeks

⅓ cup dry white wine or chicken broth

¼ cup sliced almonds

1 tablespoon grated Parmesan cheese

1. Heat oven to 375°.

2. If fish fillets are large, cut into 4 serving pieces. Arrange in ungreased square baking dish, 8 × 8 × 2 inches. Sprinkle with paprika, salt and pepper.

3. Melt butter in 10-inch skillet over medium heat. Cook mushrooms and leeks in butter, stirring occasionally, until leeks are tender. Stir in wine. Pour mushroom mixture over fish. Sprinkle with almonds and cheese.

4. Bake uncovered 15 to 20 minutes or until fish flakes easily with fork.

1 serving: Calories 170 (Calories from Fat 70); Fat 8g (Saturated 3g); Cholesterol 60mg; Sodium 420mg; Carbohydrate 3g (Dietary Fiber 1g); Protein 20g

Betty's Tip

Baking fish with the skin on helps to hold delicate fish fillets together. Removing the skin after the fish has been cooked is much easier than removing it before cooking. When the fish is done, carefully insert a metal spatula between the skin and the flesh, starting at the tail end if the fillet happens to have one. While holding on to a small piece of skin, slide the fish off of the skin.

MAKE IT A MEAL

Serve the flounder and sauce on a bed of buttered spinach noodles with a fresh tomato-basil salad on the side.

Grilled Lemon-Garlic Halibut Steaks with Pea Pods

4 SERVINGS PREP TIME: **20 MINUTES** START TO FINISH: **43 MINUTES**

¼ cup lemon juice

1 tablespoon olive oil

¼ teaspoon salt

¼ teaspoon pepper

2 cloves garlic, finely chopped

4 halibut or tuna steaks, about 1 inch thick (about 2 pounds)

¼ cup chopped fresh parsley

1 tablespoon grated lemon peel

2 cups snow (Chinese) pea pods, strings removed

Betty's Tips

You will need 1 large lemon for 1 tablespoon grated lemon peel and ¼ cup of juice. Room-temperature lemons will yield more juice than those that are cold.

1. Brush grill rack with canola oil. Heat coals or gas grill. Mix lemon juice, oil, salt, pepper and garlic in shallow glass or plastic dish or resealable plastic food-storage bag. Add halibut and turn several times to coat. Cover dish or seal bag and refrigerate 10 minutes.

2. Remove fish from dish or bag and reserve marinade. Place fish on grill and cover grill. Cook over medium heat 9 to 13 minutes, turning once and brushing with marinade, until fish flakes easily with fork (tuna will be slightly pink in center). Discard any remaining marinade. Sprinkle fish with parsley and lemon peel. Cover with aluminum foil to keep warm.

3. Meanwhile, heat 1 inch water to boiling in 1-quart saucepan over high heat. Add pea pods. Cook 2 to 3 minutes or until crisp-tender; drain. Serve fish with pea pods.

1 serving: Calories 210 (Calories from Fat 50); Fat 6g (Saturated 1g); Cholesterol 100mg; Sodium 310mg; Carbohydrate 4g (Dietary Fiber 1g); Protein 36g

Parmesan-Basil Perch

4 SERVINGS PREP TIME: **10 MINUTES** START TO FINISH: **30 MINUTES**

2 tablespoons dry bread crumbs

2 tablespoons grated Parmesan cheese

1 tablespoon chopped fresh or 1 teaspoon dried basil leaves

½ teaspoon paprika

Dash of pepper

1 pound ocean perch or other lean fish fillets, cut into 4 serving pieces

1 tablespoon margarine, melted

1 tablespoon chopped fresh parsley

1. Move oven rack to position slightly above middle of oven. Heat oven to 375°. Spray rectangular pan, 13 × 9 × 2 inches, with cooking spray.

2. Mix bread crumbs, cheese, basil, paprika and pepper. Brush one side of fish with margarine, then dip into crumb mixture. Place fish, coated sides up, in pan. Bake uncovered 15 to 20 minutes or until fish flakes easily with fork. Sprinkle with parsley.

1 serving: Calories 145 (Calories from Fat 45); Fat 5g (Saturated 1g); Cholesterol 60mg; Sodium 180mg; Carbohydrate 3g (Dietary Fiber 0g); Protein 22g

MAKE IT A MEAL
White and Green Beans

4 SERVINGS PREP TIME: **5 MINUTES** START TO FINISH: **20 MINUTES**

1 pound green beans, cut into 1- to 1½-inch pieces

2 tablespoons margarine or butter, melted

1 tablespoon lemon juice

2 teaspoons Dijon mustard

2 teaspoons honey

½ teaspoon lemon-pepper seasoning

¼ teaspoon salt

1 can (15 to 16 ounces) great northern or navy beans, rinsed and drained

1. Boil green beans uncovered in 3-quart saucepan 5 to 10 minutes or until crisp-tender; drain.

2. Stir in remaining ingredients. Cook over medium heat about 5 minutes, stirring occasionally, until hot.

1 serving: Calories 134 (Calories from Fat 51); Fat 6g (Saturated 1g); Cholesterol 0mg; Sodium 619mg; Carbohydrate 21g (Dietary Fiber 8g); Protein 5g

Broiled Salmon with Orange-Mustard Glaze

4 SERVINGS PREP TIME: **5 MINUTES** START TO FINISH: **20 MINUTES**

1 pound salmon fillets, cut into 4 pieces

2 tablespoons orange marmalade

2 teaspoons mustard seed

¼ teaspoon salt

⅛ teaspoon red pepper sauce

1. Set oven control to broil. Spray broiler pan rack with cooking spray. Place salmon, skin side down, on rack in broiler pan. Broil with tops 4 inches from heat 10 to 15 minutes or until fish flakes easily with fork.

2. Meanwhile, mix remaining ingredients in small bowl. Spread on salmon during last 5 minutes of broiling.

1 serving: Calories 190 (Calories from Fat 60); Fat 7g (Saturated 2g); Cholesterol 75mg; Sodium 220mg; Carbohydrate 7g (Dietary Fiber 0g); Protein 25g

MAKE IT A MEAL

Serve with sweet green peas and buttered new potatoes sprinkled with parsley.

Quinoa Pilaf with Salmon and Asparagus

4 SERVINGS PREP TIME: **15 MINUTES** START TO FINISH: **40 MINUTES**

1 cup uncooked quinoa

6 cups water

1 vegetable bouillon cube

1 pound salmon fillets

2 tablespoons butter or margarine

20 stalks fresh asparagus, cut diagonally into 2-inch pieces (2 cups)

4 medium green onions, sliced (¼ cup)

1 cup frozen sweet peas, thawed

½ cup halved grape tomatoes

½ cup vegetable or chicken broth

1 teaspoon lemon-pepper seasoning

2 teaspoons chopped fresh or ½ teaspoon dried dill weed

Betty's Tips

Quinoa (keen-wa) is an ancient grain native to South America. Quinoa is higher in protein than most grains and is actually a complete protein.

Vegetable broth and chicken broth are available in convenient 32-ounce resealable cartons. Cooking grains in broth adds flavor and pizzazz to your recipes.

1. Rinse quinoa thoroughly by placing in a fine-mesh strainer and holding under cold running water until water runs clear; drain well.

2. Heat 2 cups of the water to boiling in 2-quart saucepan over high heat. Add quinoa and reduce heat to low. Cover and simmer 10 to 12 minutes or until water is absorbed.

3. Meanwhile, heat remaining 4 cups water and bouillon cube to boiling in 12-inch skillet over high heat. Add salmon, skin side up, and reduce heat to low. Cover and simmer 10 to 12 minutes or until fish flakes easily with fork. Remove with slotted spoon to plate; let cool. Discard water. Remove skin from salmon and break into large pieces.

4. Meanwhile, rinse and dry the skillet. Melt butter in skillet over medium heat. Add asparagus and cook 5 minutes, stirring frequently. Stir in onions and cook 1 minute, stirring frequently. Stir in peas, tomatoes and broth and cook 1 minute.

5. Gently stir quinoa, salmon, lemon-pepper and dill weed into asparagus mixture. Cover and cook about 2 minutes or until thoroughly heated.

1 serving: Calories 420 (Calories from Fat 140); Fat 15g (Saturated 6g); Cholesterol 90mg; Sodium 650mg; Carbohydrate 37g (Dietary Fiber 5g); Protein 34g

Lemon-Dill Salmon and Potatoes

4 SERVINGS PREP TIME: **10 MINUTES** START TO FINISH: **33 MINUTES**

1 pound salmon fillets, cut into ¾-inch pieces

½ teaspoon lemon-pepper seasoning

1 tablespoon margarine, butter or spread

6 to 8 small red potatoes, cut into fourths (2 cups)

¼ cup water

½ cup frozen green peas

2 tablespoons lemon juice

1 tablespoon chopped fresh or 1 teaspoon dried dill weed

1. Sprinkle salmon pieces with ¼ teaspoon of the lemon-pepper.

2. Melt margarine in 12-inch nonstick skillet over medium-high heat. Cook salmon in margarine 3 to 5 minutes, stirring occasionally, until salmon flakes easily with fork. Remove salmon from skillet.

3. Heat potatoes and water to boiling in same skillet. Reduce heat to medium-low. Cover and cook 5 to 8 minutes or until potatoes are tender. Stir in peas. Cook 3 minutes.

4. Stir in lemon juice, dill weed, remaining ¼ teaspoon lemon-pepper and the salmon. Cook 3 to 5 minutes, stirring occasionally, until hot.

1 serving: Calories 315 (Calories from Fat 80); Fat 9g (Saturated 2g); Cholesterol 65mg; Sodium 160mg; Carbohydrate 38g (Dietary Fiber 4g); Protein 24g

MAKE IT A MEAL

For a shortcut salad, purchase packaged lettuce mixes with dressing and croutons included.

Glazed Salmon with Apples

6 SERVINGS PREP TIME: **10 MINUTES** START TO FINISH: **35 MINUTES**

2 large apples, sliced

1 small onion, peeled and sliced

1 salmon fillet (1½ pounds)

2 tablespoons Dijon mustard

1 tablespoon honey

¼ teaspoon garlic salt

1. Heat oven to 400°. Mix apples and onion in ungreased rectangular baking dish, 11 × 7 × 1½ inches. Place salmon, skin side down, on apple mixture. Mix mustard, honey and garlic salt. Spoon onto fish and spread evenly.

2. Bake uncovered 20 to 25 minutes or until salmon flakes easily with fork. Serve apple mixture with salmon.

1 serving: Calories 190 (Calories from Fat 55); Fat 6g (Saturated 2g); Cholesterol 65mg; Sodium 160mg; Carbohydrate 15g (Dietary Fiber 2g); Protein 21g

MAKE IT A MEAL

Seasoned rice from a mix and steamed broccoli go perfectly with this supper.

Lemon and Herb Salmon Packets

4 SERVINGS PREP TIME: **15 MINUTES** START TO FINISH: **35 MINUTES**

2 cups uncooked instant rice

1 can (14 ounces) chicken broth

1 cup matchstick-cut carrots

4 salmon fillets (4 to 6 ounces each)

1 teaspoon lemon-pepper seasoning

½ teaspoon salt

⅓ cup chopped fresh chives

1 medium lemon, cut lengthwise in half, then cut crosswise into ¼-inch slices

Betty's Tip

In place of chives, use whatever fresh herbs you have on hand. Basil, parsley or thyme would all taste delicious with the salmon.

1. Heat coals or gas grill for direct heat. Cut four 18 × 12-inch sheets of heavy-duty aluminum foil. Spray with cooking spray. Mix rice and broth in medium bowl. Let stand about 5 minutes or until most of broth is absorbed. Stir in carrots.

2. Place a salmon fillet on one side of each foil sheet. Sprinkle with lemon-pepper and salt. Top with chives. Arrange lemon slices over salmon. Spoon one-fourth of the rice mixture around each fillet.

3. Fold foil over salmon and rice so edges meet. Seal edges, making tight ½-inch fold; fold again. Allow space on sides for circulation and expansion.

4. Cover and grill packets 4 to 6 inches from low heat 11 to 14 minutes or until salmon flakes easily with fork. Place packets on plates. Cut a large × shape across top of each packet and fold back foil.

1 serving: Calories 400 (Calories from Fat 70); Fat 8g (Saturated 2g); Cholesterol 75mg; Sodium 1,160mg; Carbohydrate 51g (Dietary Fiber 2g); Protein 31g

Salmon with Ginger-Citrus Salsa

4 SERVINGS PREP TIME: **30 MINUTES** START TO FINISH: **2 HOURS 45 MINUTES**

SALMON

1 lemon

4 cups water

6 thin slices gingerroot

½ teaspoon salt

¼ teaspoon coarsely ground pepper

1 pound salmon fillets, cut into 4 pieces

SALSA

2 navel oranges, peeled and finely chopped

1 lime, peeled and finely chopped

½ cup chopped red bell pepper

2 tablespoons chopped fresh chives

1 tablespoon honey

1 teaspoon grated gingerroot

1 teaspoon olive oil

SPEED SUPPER

The salsa can be prepared and refrigerated in a tightly covered container for up to 24 hours before serving.

1. Grate enough peel from lemon to make 2 teaspoons and set aside for salsa. Cut lemon into slices. In 10- or 12-inch skillet, heat lemon slices, water, sliced gingerroot, salt and pepper to boiling. Boil 3 minutes, then reduce heat to medium-low.

2. Add salmon, skin side down, to skillet. Cover and cook 7 to 10 minutes or until salmon flakes easily with fork. Carefully remove salmon with slotted spoon and place in square baking dish, 8 × 8 × 2 inches. Cover and refrigerate at least 2 hours but no longer than 24 hours. Discard liquid mixture in skillet.

3. Mix oranges, lime, bell pepper, chives, honey, grated gingerroot, oil and reserved 2 teaspoons lemon peel in medium glass or plastic bowl.

4. To serve, carefully remove skin from salmon and place salmon on serving plate. Spoon salsa over salmon, using slotted spoon.

1 serving: Calories 240 (Calories from Fat 70); Fat 8g (Saturated 2g); Cholesterol 75mg; Sodium 370mg; Carbohydrate 17g (Dietary Fiber 3g); Protein 25g

MAKE IT A MEAL

Serve with warm tortillas.

Salmon-Pasta Toss

4 SERVINGS PREP TIME: **15 MINUTES** START TO FINISH: **25 MINUTES**

8 ounces uncooked linguine

1 tablespoon olive oil

12 ounces skinless salmon fillets, cut into 1-inch pieces

1 cup sliced mushrooms

12 asparagus spears, cut into 1-inch pieces

2 cloves garlic, finely chopped

¼ cup chopped fresh or 2 teaspoons dried basil leaves

12 grape tomatoes

2 medium green onions, sliced (2 tablespoons)

4 teaspoons cornstarch

1 cup chicken broth

¼ cup shredded Parmesan cheese

1. Cook and drain pasta as directed on package, omitting salt.

2. While pasta is cooking, heat oil in 12-inch nonstick skillet over medium heat. Cook salmon in oil 4 to 5 minutes, stirring gently and frequently, until salmon flakes easily with fork (salmon may break apart). Remove from skillet.

3. Increase heat to medium-high. Add mushrooms, asparagus and garlic to skillet. Cook and stir 2 minutes. Stir in basil, tomatoes and onions. Cook and stir 1 minute longer.

4. Stir cornstarch into broth in 2-cup glass measuring cup. Add to vegetable mixture. Cook and stir 1 to 2 minutes or until sauce is thickened and bubbly. Stir in salmon. Serve over linguine. Sprinkle with cheese.

1 serving: Calories 440 (Calories from Fat 110); Fat 12g (Saturated 3g); Cholesterol 60mg; Sodium 410mg; Carbohydrate 52g (Dietary Fiber 5g); Protein 32g

Betty's Tip

If the salmon you purchased has skin, remove the skin before cutting the salmon into pieces. Place the fillet, skin side down, on a cutting board. Using a sharp knife, cut between the flesh and skin, angling knife down toward the skin and using a sawing motion. Grip the skin tightly with your other hand after a small portion has been removed.

Sole with Almonds

4 SERVINGS PREP TIME: **10 MINUTES** START TO FINISH: **30 MINUTES**

1 pound sole or other lean fish fillets, about ¾ inch thick

⅓ cup sliced almonds or chopped walnuts

3 tablespoons margarine or butter, at room temperature

1½ tablespoons grated lemon peel

1½ tablespoons lemon juice

½ teaspoon salt

½ teaspoon paprika

1. Heat oven to 375°. Grease bottom of square pan, 8 × 8 × 2 inches, with oil.

2. If fish fillets are large, cut into 4 serving pieces. Place pieces, skin sides down, in greased pan.

3. Mix almonds, margarine, lemon peel, lemon juice, salt and paprika. Spoon over fish.

4. Bake uncovered 15 to 20 minutes or until fish flakes easily with fork.

1 serving: Calories 220 (Calories from Fat 125); Fat 14g (Saturated 2g); Cholesterol 55mg; Sodium 480mg; Carbohydrate 3g (Dietary Fiber 1g); Protein 21g

MAKE IT A MEAL
Oven-Roasted Vegetables

6 SERVINGS PREP TIME: **10 MINUTES** START TO FINISH: **35 MINUTES**

1⅓ cups 1-inch chunks unpeeled baking potatoes (2 medium)

1 cup 1-inch chunks unpeeled sweet potato (1 medium)

2 medium onions, cut crosswise in half, then cut into wedges

⅓ cup fat-free Italian dressing

¼ teaspoon ground red pepper (cayenne)

1 medium bell pepper, cut into 1-inch squares

1. Move oven rack to position slightly above middle of oven. Heat oven to 500°.

2. Generously spray rectangular pan, 13 × 9 × 2 inches, with cooking spray. Place baking potatoes, sweet potato and onions in pan. Mix dressing and red pepper and pour over vegetables. Cover and bake 10 minutes.

3. Stir bell pepper into vegetables. Cover and bake 5 minutes. Stir vegetables. Bake uncovered 10 minutes longer.

1 serving: Calories 80 (Calories from Fat 0); Fat 0g (Saturated 0g); Cholesterol 0mg; Sodium 125mg; Carbohydrate 21g (Dietary Fiber 3g); Protein 2g

SPEED SUPPER
Roasting the potatoes with their skins on not only saves time but also provides more fiber, iron, calcium and B vitamins.

Grilled Swordfish with Black Bean and Corn Salsa

6 SERVINGS PREP TIME: **20 MINUTES** START TO FINISH: **1 HOUR 10 MINUTES**

SWORDFISH

1 teaspoon finely grated lime peel

3 tablespoons lime juice

½ teaspoon ground cumin

¼ teaspoon salt

⅛ teaspoon pepper

2 cloves garlic, finely chopped

Liquid from diced tomatoes used in salsa (about ½ cup)

3 swordfish steaks (10 to 12 ounces each), cut in half

SALSA

1 can (15 ounces) Southwestern black beans, drained and rinsed

1 can (11 ounces) whole kernel corn, drained

1 can (10 ounces) diced tomatoes with green chilies, drained, liquid reserved

4 medium green onions, chopped (¼ cup)

1 tablespoon olive oil

2 teaspoons dry sherry or red wine vinegar

¼ teaspoon salt

⅛ teaspoon pepper

1. Mix all swordfish ingredients except the swordfish in shallow glass or plastic dish. Add swordfish and turn to coat with marinade. Cover and refrigerate at least 30 minutes but no longer than 2 hours.

2. Meanwhile, mix all salsa ingredients in medium bowl. Let stand at room temperature.

3. Spray grill rack with cooking spray. Heat coals or gas grill. Remove swordfish from dish and reserve marinade. Place fish on grill and cover grill. Cook over medium heat 15 to 20 minutes, brushing 2 or 3 times with marinade and turning once, until fish flakes easily with fork. Discard any remaining marinade. Serve fish with salsa.

1 serving: Calories 310 (Calories from Fat 90); Fat 10g (Saturated 2g); Cholesterol 75mg; Sodium 680mg; Carbohydrate 25g (Dietary Fiber 7g); Protein 31g

SPEED SUPPER
To save time, the swordfish can be refrigerated in the marinade for 15 minutes.

Tilapia Florentine

4 SERVINGS PREP TIME: **18 MINUTES** START TO FINISH: **30 MINUTES**

4 tilapia or other mild-flavored fish fillets
(5 ounces each)

⅓ cup reduced-fat mayonnaise or salad
dressing

2 teaspoons lemon juice

1 teaspoon Dijon mustard

½ teaspoon dried tarragon leaves

¼ teaspoon lemon-pepper seasoning

4 teaspoons garlic-herb dry bread crumbs

2 teaspoons olive oil

1½ cups sliced mushrooms (4 ounces)

1 tablespoon lemon juice

6 cups lightly packed washed fresh spinach
leaves (9 ounces)

½ teaspoon salt

Betty's Tip

Tilapia is a very popular fish with a mild flavor
that pairs well with tarragon. If you like
tarragon, you're in for a treat. Not a tarragon
lover? You may want to cut back a bit on the
amount.

1. Heat oven to 450°. Spray rectangular pan, 11 × 7 × 1½ inches, with cooking spray.

2. Place tilapia fillets in pan. Mix mayonnaise, 2 teaspoons lemon juice, the mustard, tarragon and lemon-pepper in small bowl until blended. Spread mayonnaise mixture evenly over fillets. Sprinkle with bread crumbs.

3. Bake 10 to 12 minutes or until fish flakes easily with fork.

4. Meanwhile, heat oil in 12-inch skillet over medium heat. Cook mushrooms in oil about 5 minutes, stirring occasionally, until softened. Stir in 1 tablespoon lemon juice. Gradually stir in spinach. Cook about 3 minutes, stirring occasionally, just until spinach is wilted. Sprinkle with salt.

5. To serve, place spinach on each tilapia fillet.

1 serving: Calories 240 (Calories from Fat 100); Fat 11g (Saturated 2g); Cholesterol 80mg; Sodium 680mg; Carbohydrate 7g (Dietary Fiber 2g); Protein 29g

Sautéed Tuna with Creamy Tarragon Sauce

6 SERVINGS PREP TIME: **5 MINUTES** START TO FINISH: **25 MINUTES**

6 small yellowfin tuna, grouper or
sea bass steaks, about 1 inch thick
(about 1½ pounds)

¾ cup apple juice

3 tablespoons reduced-fat sour cream

2 tablespoons chopped fresh or 2 teaspoons
dried tarragon leaves

¼ teaspoon ground mustard

Betty's Tip

Tuna is moderately high in fat, firm in texture
and stronger in flavor than many other types
of fish. Fresh tuna is key in this recipe. Give it
a try!

1. Spray 10-inch nonstick skillet with cooking spray and heat over medium-high heat. Cook tuna in skillet 5 minutes; turn. Cover and cook 5 to 6 minutes longer or until tuna flakes easily with fork. Remove from skillet and keep warm.

2. Mix remaining ingredients in small bowl and add to skillet. Heat to boiling. Boil 5 to 6 minutes or until reduced to ½ cup. Serve over fish.

1 serving: Calories 130 (Calories from Fat 20); Fat 2g (Saturated 1g); Cholesterol 65mg; Sodium 110mg; Carbohydrate 5g (Dietary Fiber 0g); Protein 23g

MAKE IT A MEAL

Serve with steamed broccoli and a hearty, toothsome bread such as seven-grain or peasant sourdough.

Tuna with Avocado-Kiwi Salsa

6 SERVINGS PREP TIME: **20 MINUTES** START TO FINISH: **1 HOUR 6 MINUTES**

TUNA

1½ pounds tuna steaks, ¾ to 1 inch thick

¼ cup lime juice

2 teaspoons chili oil

2 tablespoons finely chopped fresh cilantro

1 clove garlic, finely chopped

½ teaspoon salt

SALSA

1 small avocado, pitted, peeled and coarsely chopped (1 cup)

1 kiwifruit, peeled and chopped (½ cup)

3 medium green onions, chopped (3 tablespoons)

1 medium jalapeño chili, seeded and finely chopped (1 tablespoon)

2 tablespoons lime juice

2 tablespoons chopped fresh cilantro

¼ teaspoon salt

1. If tuna steaks are large, cut into 6 serving pieces. Mix lime juice, chili oil, cilantro, garlic and salt in shallow glass or plastic dish. Add tuna and turn to coat with marinade. Cover and refrigerate, turning once, at least 30 minutes but no longer than 2 hours.

2. Meanwhile, mix all salsa ingredients in medium bowl; refrigerate.

3. Spray grill rack with cooking spray. Heat coals or gas grill. Remove tuna from dish and reserve marinade. Place tuna on grill and cover grill. Cook over medium heat 11 to 16 minutes, brushing 2 or 3 times with marinade and turning once, until tuna flakes easily with fork and is slightly pink in center. Discard any remaining marinade. Top tuna with salsa.

1 serving: Calories 210 (Calories from Fat 100); Fat 11g (Saturated 2.5g); Cholesterol 65mg; Sodium 360mg; Carbohydrate 6g (Dietary Fiber 2g); Protein 23g

SPEED SUPPER
To save time, the tuna can be refrigerated in the marinade for 15 minutes.

Betty's Tip
This lovely tuna, with the refreshing flavors of lime, avocado and kiwi, is equal to any restaurant menu item and is a terrific way to enjoy fish.

MAKE IT A MEAL
Serve with hot basmati rice.

Walleye with Dill and Lemon-Pepper Vegetables

4 SERVINGS PREP TIME: **10 MINUTES** START TO FINISH: **25 MINUTES**

1 pound walleye, haddock or other lean fish fillets, ½ inch thick

1 can (14½ ounces) chicken broth

1 small red onion, cut lengthwise in half, then cut crosswise into thin slices

2 teaspoons lemon-pepper seasoning

½ teaspoon dried dill weed

1 bag (1 pound) frozen baby peas, carrots, snow pea pods and baby corn cobs, thawed

2 tablespoons cornstarch

Hot cooked fettuccine, if desired

1. Cut walleye into 4 serving pieces.

2. Reserve 2 tablespoons of the broth. Heat remaining broth, the onion, lemon-pepper and dill weed to boiling in 12-inch nonstick skillet; reduce heat. Cover and simmer about 3 minutes or until onion is tender.

3. Stir in vegetables. Arrange fish in vegetable mixture. Heat to boiling, then reduce heat to medium. Cover and cook about 4 minutes or until fish flakes easily with fork.

4. Carefully remove fish from skillet, using wide slotted spatula. Mix reserved broth and the cornstarch and stir into vegetable mixture. Heat to boiling, stirring constantly. Boil and stir 1 minute. Serve fish and vegetables over fettuccine if desired.

1 serving: Calories 190 (Calories from Fat 20); Fat 2g (Saturated 0g); Cholesterol 65mg; Sodium 510mg; Carbohydrate 21g (Dietary Fiber 5g); Protein 27g

MAKE IT A MEAL

Serve fresh fruit or sherbet for dessert.

Creole Mustard-Broiled Whitefish

6 SERVINGS PREP TIME: **10 MINUTES** START TO FINISH: **18 MINUTES**

6 whitefish, swordfish or other medium-fat fish steaks, about ¾ inch thick (about 1¼ pounds)

⅔ cup reduced-fat mayonnaise or salad dressing

1 tablespoon chopped fresh chives

1 tablespoon Creole mustard or spicy brown mustard

½ teaspoon reduced-sodium Worcestershire sauce

⅛ teaspoon pepper

1. Set oven control to broil. Spray broiler pan rack with cooking spray. Place whitefish on rack in broiler pan. Broil with tops about 4 inches from heat 5 minutes.

2. While fish is broiling, mix remaining ingredients. Carefully turn fish, using wide slotted spatula. Spread mayonnaise mixture over tops of fish. Broil about 3 minutes or until fish flakes easily with fork.

1 serving: Calories 305 (Calories from Fat 170); Fat 19g (Saturated 3g); Cholesterol 95mg; Sodium 300mg; Carbohydrate 2g (Dietary Fiber 0g); Protein 31g

Betty's Tip

One of the favorite seasonings of Louisiana's German-Creole cooks, Creole mustard is spicy-hot with a whisper of horseradish. Look for it in food specialty shops or the mustard aisle of your supermarket.

MAKE IT A MEAL

Cook 3 cups sliced carrots in boiling water for 5 minutes or until crisp-tender. Drain and return to pan. Add 2 tablespoons packed brown sugar, 2 tablespoons margarine or butter, and ½ teaspoon ground ginger. Cook, stirring occasionally, for 2 to 4 minutes, or until carrots are glazed.

Italian Tuna Toss

6 TO 8 SERVINGS PREP TIME: **10 MINUTES** START TO FINISH: **10 MINUTES**

1 bag (10 ounces) salad mix (about 8 cups)

1 bag (1 pound) fresh cauliflowerets

1 medium cucumber, sliced

2 cans (6 ounces each) tuna in water, drained

1 jar (2 ounces) sliced pimientos, drained

⅓ cup Italian dressing

¼ cup bacon flavor bits or chips

Toss all ingredients except dressing and bacon bits in large bowl. Add dressing and bacon bits; toss.

1 serving: Calories 175 (Calories from Fat 65); Fat 7g (Saturated 1g); Cholesterol 20mg; Sodium 400mg; Carbohydrate 9g (Dietary Fiber 4g); Protein 19g

MAKE IT A MEAL

Warm slices of purchased focaccia bread in the toaster oven or oven.

Halibut and Asparagus Stir-Fry

4 SERVINGS PREP TIME: 10 MINUTES START TO FINISH: 15 MINUTES

1 pound halibut, swordfish or tuna fillets, cut into 1-inch pieces

1 medium onion, thinly sliced

3 cloves garlic, finely chopped

1 teaspoon finely chopped gingerroot

1 package (10 ounces) frozen asparagus cuts, thawed and drained

1 package (8 ounces) sliced mushrooms (3 cups)

1 medium tomato, cut into thin wedges

2 tablespoons reduced-sodium soy sauce

1 tablespoon lemon juice

1. Spray 10-inch nonstick skillet with cooking spray and heat over medium-high heat. Add halibut, onion, garlic, gingerroot and asparagus. Stir-fry 2 to 3 minutes or until fish almost flakes with fork.

2. Carefully stir in remaining ingredients. Cook until heated through and fish flakes easily with fork. Serve with additional reduced-sodium soy sauce if desired.

1 serving: Calories 180 (Calories from Fat 20); Fat 2g (Saturated 1g); Cholesterol 75mg; Sodium 390mg; Carbohydrate 11g (Dietary Fiber 3g); Protein 32g

Spicy Fish Stew

4 SERVINGS PREP TIME: **5 MINUTES** START TO FINISH: **27 MINUTES**

½ cup clam juice

4 cloves garlic, finely chopped

3 cups packaged fresh stir-fry vegetables

½ pound cod fillets, cubed

1½ tablespoons chopped fresh (seeded) or canned jalapeño chilies

2 tablespoons fish sauce or reduced-sodium soy sauce

1 tablespoon packed brown sugar

4 cups hot cooked rice

1. Heat ¼ cup of the clam juice to boiling in 10-inch nonstick skillet. Cook garlic in clam juice 1 minute.

2. Stir in stir-fry vegetables. Cook about 8 minutes, stirring frequently, until liquid has evaporated.

3. Stir in cod, chilies, fish sauce, brown sugar and remaining ¼ cup clam juice. Heat to boiling, then reduce heat to medium. Cook uncovered 10 minutes. Serve with rice.

1 serving: Calories 305 (Calories from Fat 10); Fat 1g (Saturated 0g); Cholesterol 30mg; Sodium 610mg; Carbohydrate 56g (Dietary Fiber 2g); Protein 18g

Betty's Tip

Mix up the flavor of this sweet and spicy stew by experimenting with different kinds of fish. Halibut, orange roughy or haddock will all taste great.

Grilled Fish Tacos

4 SERVINGS PREP TIME: **20 MINUTES** START TO FINISH: **56 MINUTES**

2 tablespoons lime juice

2 teaspoons chili powder

1 teaspoon ground cumin

2 tilapia or cod fillets (5 ounces each)

4 whole wheat tortillas (6 inches in diameter)

1 cup shredded lettuce

½ cup black beans (from 15-ounce can), drained and rinsed

¼ cup chopped seeded tomato

¼ cup shredded reduced-fat Cheddar cheese (1 ounce)

¼ cup fat-free sour cream, if desired

2 tablespoons chopped fresh cilantro

1. Mix lime juice, chili powder and cumin in heavy-duty resealable plastic food-storage bag. Add tilapia and seal bag. Turn bag several times to coat fish with marinade. Refrigerate 15 to 30 minutes.

2. Brush grill rack with canola oil. Heat coals or gas grill. Place fish on grill and cover grill. Cook over medium heat 4 to 6 minutes, turning after 2 minutes, until fish flakes easily with fork.

3. Cut fish into bite-size pieces and divide among tortillas. Fill with lettuce, beans, tomato, cheese, sour cream (if desired) and cilantro.

1 serving: Calories 170 (Calories from Fat 20); Fat 2.5g (Saturated 0.5g); Cholesterol 40mg; Sodium 240mg; Carbohydrate 17g (Dietary Fiber 4g); Protein 19g

SPEED SUPPER

Shave time by refrigerating the fish in the marinade for only 15 minutes.

MAKE IT A MEAL

Toss a big Caesar salad to serve alongside these tasty tacos.

Cuban-Style Tilapia Salad

4 SERVINGS PREP TIME: **22 MINUTES** START TO FINISH: **30 MINUTES**

DRESSING

½ cup pineapple juice

1 teaspoon grated lime peel

2 tablespoons lime juice

1 tablespoon canola oil

TILAPIA SALAD

4 tilapia or other mild-flavored fish fillets (about 5 ounces each)

Cooking spray

2 tablespoons lime juice

¼ teaspoon seasoned salt

4 cups mixed salad greens

2 cups fresh or canned (drained) pineapple chunks

¼ cup fresh mint leaves

1. Beat all dressing ingredients in 1-cup glass measuring cup with wire whisk.

2. Set oven control to broil. Place tilapia on rack in broiler pan. Spray tops of fish with cooking spray. Sprinkle tops of fish with 2 tablespoons lime juice and the seasoned salt. Broil with tops 4 to 6 inches from heat 6 to 8 minutes or until fish flakes easily with fork.

3. Meanwhile, arrange 1 cup salad greens on each of 4 plates. Divide pineapple among plates. Place fish on or next to greens. Sprinkle greens and fish with mint. Serve with dressing.

1 serving: Calories 230 (Calories from Fat 50); Fat 5g (Saturated 0.5g); Cholesterol 75mg; Sodium 390mg; Carbohydrate 17g (Dietary Fiber 2g); Protein 28g

MAKE IT A MEAL

Drain and rinse 1 cup canned black beans. Divide the beans among the plates with the greens. Serve with whole grain bread and skim milk.

Mediterranean Shrimp with Bulgur

6 SERVINGS PREP TIME: **25 MINUTES** START TO FINISH: **40 MINUTES**

2 cups water

1 cup uncooked bulgur

2 teaspoons olive oil

1 medium onion, chopped (½ cup)

¼ cup dry white wine or nonalcoholic wine

2 cans (14½ ounces each) diced tomatoes with basil, oregano and garlic, undrained

3 tablespoons chopped fresh parsley

1 tablespoon capers, drained

¼ teaspoon black pepper

⅛ teaspoon crushed red pepper

1 pound uncooked peeled deveined small shrimp

½ cup crumbled reduced-fat feta cheese (2 ounces)

1. Heat water to boiling in 2-quart saucepan. Add bulgur and reduce heat to low. Cover and simmer about 12 minutes or until water is absorbed.

2. Meanwhile, heat oil in 12-inch skillet over medium heat. Add onion and cook about 4 minutes, stirring occasionally, until tender. Stir in wine and cook 1 minute, stirring frequently.

3. Stir tomatoes, 1½ tablespoons of the parsley, the capers, black pepper and red pepper into onion. Cook 3 minutes. Stir in shrimp. Cover and cook 4 to 5 minutes or until shrimp are pink.

4. Stir cooked bulgur into shrimp mixture. Sprinkle with cheese. Cover and cook 2 minutes. Sprinkle with remaining 1½ tablespoons parsley.

1 serving: Calories 210 (Calories from Fat 35); Fat 4g (Saturated 1.5g); Cholesterol 110mg; Sodium 480mg; Carbohydrate 25g (Dietary Fiber 6g); Protein 18g

Betty's Tip

If you cannot find diced tomatoes with basil, oregano and garlic, use plain diced tomatoes and add 1 teaspoon each of finely chopped fresh garlic, dried oregano and dried basil.

Quick Paella

4 SERVINGS PREP TIME: **10 MINUTES** START TO FINISH: **20 MINUTES**

¼ cup margarine or butter

1⅓ cups uncooked instant rice

1 medium onion, finely chopped (½ cup)

⅓ cup chopped green bell pepper

2 cloves garlic, finely chopped

1½ cups water

2 cans (8 ounces each) tomato sauce

1 can (6½ ounces) minced clams, drained

1 can (5 ounces) chunk chicken

Pinch of saffron or turmeric, if desired

1. Melt margarine in 10-inch skillet over medium heat. Cook rice, onion, bell pepper and garlic in margarine, stirring occasionally, until rice is light brown.

2. Stir in remaining ingredients. Heat to boiling; reduce heat. Simmer uncovered about 5 minutes or until rice is tender.

1 serving: Calories 332 (Calories from Fat 115); Fat 13g (Saturated 3g); Cholesterol 37mg; Sodium 1,020mg; Carbohydrate 38g (Dietary Fiber 3g); Protein 16g

MAKE IT A MEAL

Paella is really a meal in itself. Offer refreshing lemon sherbet and shortbread cookies for dessert.

Corn 'n Crab Cakes

4 SERVINGS PREP TIME: **20 MINUTES** START TO FINISH: **1 HOUR**

½ cup frozen whole kernel corn, thawed

4 medium green onions, chopped (¼ cup)

⅓ cup fat-free mayonnaise or salad dressing

1 tablespoon 40%-less-sodium taco seasoning mix (from 1¼-ounce envelope)

2 cans (6 ounces each) crabmeat, drained and cartilage removed

1 egg or 2 egg whites

2 tablespoons water

½ cup plain dry bread crumbs

3 tablespoons chunky-style salsa

1. Line cookie sheet with waxed paper. Mix corn, onions, mayonnaise, taco seasoning mix and crabmeat in medium bowl. Shape into 8 patties, using slightly less than ¼ cup for each patty. Place on cookie sheet and freeze 15 minutes.

2. Heat oven to 450°. Spray another cookie sheet with cooking spray. Beat egg and water in shallow bowl until blended. Place bread crumbs in another shallow bowl or pie plate.

3. Dip each patty into egg mixture, coating both sides, then coat with bread crumbs. Place on sprayed cookie sheet. Bake 15 minutes; turn patties. Bake about 10 minutes longer or until golden brown. Serve with salsa.

1 serving: Calories 180 (Calories from Fat 35); Fat 3.5g (Saturated 1g); Cholesterol 120mg; Sodium 690mg; Carbohydrate 19g (Dietary Fiber 2g); Protein 19g

MAKE IT A MEAL

Cut 2 firm medium tomatoes into ¾-inch slices. Place in a single layer in a broiler pan lightly coated with olive oil. Sprinkle with grated Parmesan cheese and a little dried oregano. Drizzle lightly with olive oil. Place in the oven during the last 5 minutes that the Corn 'n Crab Cakes are baking. When the crab cakes are done, set the oven control to broil. Broil tomatoes with tops 6 inches from heat for 2 to 4 minutes or until the topping is golden and bubbly.

Southwestern Stir-Fried Shrimp

6 SERVINGS PREP TIME: **15 MINUTES** START TO FINISH: **1 HOUR 20 MINUTES**

2 tablespoons lime juice

2 teaspoons cornstarch

½ teaspoon ground cumin

¼ teaspoon salt

¼ teaspoon pepper

1½ pounds uncooked peeled deveined large shrimp, thawed if frozen

1 large yellow bell pepper, chopped (1½ cups)

1 large red bell pepper, chopped (1½ cups)

1 medium onion, chopped (½ cup)

⅓ cup chicken broth

2 cloves garlic, finely chopped

⅛ teaspoon ground red pepper (cayenne)

2 tablespoons chopped fresh cilantro

1. Mix lime juice, cornstarch, cumin, salt and pepper in medium glass or plastic bowl. Stir in shrimp. Cover and refrigerate 1 hour.

2. Spray 12-inch nonstick skillet with cooking spray and heat over medium heat. Add bell peppers, onion, broth, garlic, red pepper and cilantro. Stir-fry 2 minutes. Add shrimp mixture and stir-fry 3 to 4 minutes or until shrimp are pink and firm.

1 serving: Calories 65 (Calories from Fat 10); Fat 1g (Saturated 0g); Cholesterol 55mg; Sodium 220mg; Carbohydrate 9g (Dietary Fiber 2g); Protein 7g

Betty's Tip

Cumin is a frequent dinner guest in Southwestern cuisine. It has a warm, earthy flavor and pungent aroma. You are probably most familiar with its flavor from eating chili.

MAKE IT A MEAL

While the shrimp are in the refrigerator, prepare corn bread from scratch or a mix.

Grilled Seafood Salad with Shallot-Thyme Vinaigrette

6 SERVINGS PREP TIME: **30 MINUTES** START TO FINISH: **1 HOUR 10 MINUTES**

VINAIGRETTE

¼ cup balsamic vinegar

3 tablespoons olive oil

2 tablespoons white wine vinegar

1 tablespoon finely chopped shallot

1 tablespoon chopped fresh or 1 teaspoon dried thyme leaves

1 tablespoon Dijon mustard

1 tablespoon water

¼ teaspoon salt

SALAD

12 uncooked peeled deveined large shrimp, thawed if frozen

1 pound swordfish, marlin or tuna steaks, ¾ to 1 inch thick

1 medium bulb fennel, cut into wedges

10 cups bite-size pieces mixed salad greens

½ small red onion, thinly sliced

12 cherry tomatoes, cut in half

12 pitted Kalamata or ripe olives

1. Shake all vinaigrette ingredients in tightly covered container. Place shrimp and fish in shallow glass or plastic dish or heavy-duty resealable plastic food-storage bag. Add ¼ cup of the vinaigrette and turn shrimp and fish to coat. Cover dish or seal bag and refrigerate 30 minutes. Set aside remaining vinaigrette to serve with salad.

2. Heat coals or gas grill. Remove shrimp and fish from dish or bag, reserving marinade. Place fish and fennel on grill and cover grill. Cook over medium heat 5 minutes, then brush with marinade. Add shrimp and cover grill. Cook about 5 minutes, turning and brushing fish, fennel and shrimp with marinade 2 or 3 times, until shrimp are pink, fish flakes easily with fork and fennel is tender. Discard any remaining marinade.

3. Arrange salad greens on serving platter. Cut fish into bite-size pieces. Arrange fish, fennel, shrimp, onion, tomatoes, and olives on greens. Serve with reserved vinaigrette.

1 serving: Calories 210 (Calories from Fat 110); Fat 12g (Saturated 2g); Cholesterol 65mg; Sodium 350mg; Carbohydrate 9g (Dietary Fiber 4g); Protein 18g

Betty's Tip

Grilling not only adds extra flavor to your food, it's a healthy way to cook because it doesn't add extra fat. Broiling, simmering, roasting and braising are all healthy ways to cook because they don't add fat.

Calypso Shrimp with Black Bean–Citrus Salsa

4 SERVINGS PREP TIME: 20 MINUTES START TO FINISH: 2 HOURS 23 MINUTES

SHRIMP

2 teaspoons grated orange peel

¼ cup orange juice

½ teaspoon seasoned salt

4 cloves garlic, finely chopped

1 pound uncooked peeled deveined
  large shrimp

SALSA

1 can (15 ounces) black beans, rinsed and
  drained

1 medium orange, peeled, divided into
  segments and cut in half

¼ cup chunky-style salsa

2 tablespoons chopped fresh cilantro

1 teaspoon grated lime peel

2 cloves garlic, finely chopped

1 tablespoon canola oil

1. Mix orange peel, orange juice, seasoned salt and 4 cloves garlic in square baking dish, 8 × 8 × 2 inches. Add shrimp and turn to coat. Cover with plastic wrap and refrigerate up to 2 hours.

2. Mix beans, orange, salsa, cilantro, lime peel and 2 cloves garlic in medium bowl. Cover and let stand until ready to serve (or refrigerate if longer than 30 minutes).

3. Heat oil in 10-inch nonstick skillet over medium-high heat. Drain shrimp and discard marinade. Cook shrimp in oil 2 to 3 minutes, stirring frequently, until shrimp are pink.

4. Divide salsa among 4 dinner plates. Arrange shrimp around salsa.

1 serving: Calories 280 (Calories from Fat 45); Fat 5g (Saturated 0.5g); Cholesterol 160mg; Sodium 470mg; Carbohydrate 33g (Dietary Fiber 7g); Protein 26g

SPEED SUPPER

You can make this dish ahead of time. Cover and refrigerate the cooked shrimp separately from the salsa. Just before serving, arrange on plates.

Skillet Chicken Parmigiana

4 SERVINGS PREP TIME: **10 MINUTES** START TO FINISH: **25 MINUTES**

4 boneless, skinless chicken breast halves (about 1¼ pounds)

⅓ cup Italian-style dry bread crumbs

⅓ cup grated Parmesan cheese

1 egg, beaten

2 tablespoons olive or vegetable oil

2 cups tomato pasta sauce

½ cup shredded mozzarella cheese (2 ounces)

1. Flatten each chicken breast half to ¼-inch thickness between sheets of plastic wrap or waxed paper. Mix bread crumbs and Parmesan cheese. Dip chicken into egg, then coat with bread crumb mixture.

2. Heat oil in 12-inch skillet over medium heat. Cook chicken in oil 10 to 15 minutes, turning once, until juice is no longer pink when centers of thickest pieces are cut. Pour pasta sauce around chicken in saucepan and heat until hot. Sprinkle mozzarella cheese over chicken.

1 serving: Calories 414 (Calories from Fat 160); Fat 18g (Saturated 5g); Cholesterol 152mg; Sodium 990mg; Carbohydrate 18g (Dietary Fiber 2g); Protein 43g

MAKE IT A MEAL
Dilled Carrots and Pea Pods

4 SERVINGS PREP TIME: **5 MINUTES** START TO FINISH: **12 MINUTES**

1½ cups snow (Chinese) pea pods (about 5 ounces)

1½ cups baby carrots

1 tablespoon margarine or butter

2 teaspoons chopped fresh or ½ teaspoon dried dill weed

⅛ teaspoon salt

1. Snap off stem end of each pea pod and pull string across pea pod to remove it.

2. Add 1 inch water to saucepan. Cover and heat water to boiling over high heat. Add carrots. Cover and heat to boiling again; reduce heat.

Simmer covered about 4 minutes or until carrots are crisp-tender. Do not drain water.

3. Add pea pods to carrots in saucepan. Heat uncovered until water is boiling again. Continue boiling uncovered 2 to 3 minutes, stirring occasionally, until pea pods are crisp-tender. Drain carrots and pea pods, then return to saucepan.

4. Stir margarine, dill weed and salt into carrots and pea pods until margarine is melted.

1 serving: Calories 45 (Calories from Fat 25); Fat 3g (Saturated 1g); Cholesterol 0mg; Sodium 130mg; Carbohydrate 6g (Dietary Fiber 2g); Protein 1g

Grilled Lime Chicken Breasts

4 SERVINGS PREP TIME: **5 MINUTES** START TO FINISH: **30 MINUTES**

¼ cup frozen (thawed) limeade concentrate

¼ cup vegetable oil

1 teaspoon finely grated lime peel, if desired

¼ teaspoon paprika

4 boneless chicken breast halves
(about 1 pound)

1. Brush grill rack with vegetable oil. Heat coals or gas grill. Mix all ingredients except chicken.

2. Place chicken, skin sides up, on grill 4 to 6 inches from medium heat. Brush with limeade mixture.

3. Cover and grill 20 to 25 minutes, brushing frequently with limeade mixture and turning occasionally, until juice is no longer pink when centers of thickest pieces are cut. Discard any remaining limeade mixture.

1 serving: Calories 290 (Calories from Fat 133); Fat 15g (Saturated 2g); Cholesterol 66mg; Sodium 74mg; Carbohydrate 11g (Dietary Fiber 0g); Protein 26g

MAKE IT A MEAL

Purchase bagged shredded coleslaw and toss with ginger-sesame salad dressing.

Wine-Poached Chicken Breasts

4 SERVINGS PREP TIME: 5 MINUTES START TO FINISH: 18 MINUTES

4 boneless, skinless chicken breast halves (about 1 pound)

½ cup dry white wine or chicken broth

1 tablespoon lemon juice

¼ teaspoon salt

1. Remove fat from chicken. Place chicken and remaining ingredients in 10-inch nonstick skillet. Heat to boiling; reduce heat.

2. Cover and simmer about 10 minutes or until juice of chicken is no longer pink when centers of thickest pieces are cut.

1 serving: Calories 140 (Calories from Fat 35); Fat 4g (Saturated 1g); Cholesterol 70mg; Sodium 210mg; Carbohydrate 1g (Dietary Fiber 0g); Protein 25g

MAKE IT A MEAL

Complement this entrée with a side of steamed broccoli spears. Squirt a little lemon juice over the veggies, and you have a healthy and elegant meal.

Oriental Barbecued Chicken

4 SERVINGS PREP TIME: **10 MINUTES** START TO FINISH: **24 MINUTES**

4 boneless, skinless chicken breast halves (about 1 pound)

½ cup hoisin sauce

1 tablespoon sesame or vegetable oil

1 tablespoon tomato paste

½ teaspoon ground ginger

2 cloves garlic, finely chopped

*Betty's Tip*_____

Hoisin sauce, a key ingredient in Chinese cooking, is a thick paste-like blend of soy sauce, garlic, chili peppers and various spices.

1. Set oven control to broil. Remove fat from chicken. Spray broiler pan rack with cooking spray. Place chicken on rack in broiler pan. Mix remaining ingredients. Brush some of the sauce over chicken.

2. Broil chicken with tops 5 to 7 inches from heat 7 minutes. Turn and brush with sauce. Broil 7 minutes longer or until juice is no longer pink when centers of thickest pieces are cut.

3. While chicken is broiling, heat remaining sauce to boiling. Boil 1 minute. Serve with chicken.

1 serving: Calories 240 (Calories from Fat 80); Fat 9g (Saturated 2g); Cholesterol 70mg; Sodium 610mg; Carbohydrate 14g (Dietary Fiber 1g); Protein 27g

MAKE IT A MEAL

Accompany the chicken with hot rice and stir-fried pea pods with sesame seeds.

Chicken with Garlic-Ginger Sauce

6 SERVINGS PREP TIME: **10 MINUTES** START TO FINISH: **40 MINUTES**

¼ cup fat-free cholesterol-free egg product,
  2 egg whites or 1 egg

2 tablespoons water

1 cup Reduced Fat Bisquick®

¼ teaspoon garlic powder

6 small boneless, skinless chicken breast
  halves (about 1½ pounds)

  Cooking spray

4 medium cloves garlic, chopped (2 teaspoons)

1 tablespoon chopped gingerroot

4 medium green onions, chopped (¼ cup)

1 tablespoon sugar

1 tablespoon soy sauce

1 tablespoon rice vinegar

1 tablespoon cooking sherry, if desired

2 teaspoons toasted sesame oil

1. Heat oven to 425°. Spray jelly roll pan, 15½ × 10½ × 1 inch, with cooking spray. Beat egg product and water slightly. Mix Bisquick and garlic powder in separate bowl. Dip chicken into egg mixture, then coat with Bisquick mixture. Place in pan. Spray chicken with cooking spray.

2. Bake 20 minutes. Turn chicken and spray with cooking spray. Bake about 10 minutes longer or until juice is no longer pink when centers of thickest pieces are cut.

3. Spray 10-inch nonstick skillet with cooking spray and heat over medium-high heat. Cook garlic and gingerroot in skillet 2 minutes, stirring constantly. Add remaining ingredients and cook 1 minute, stirring frequently. Spoon sauce over chicken.

1 serving: Calories 220 (Calories from Fat 55); Fat 6g (Saturated 2g); Cholesterol 65mg; Sodium 440mg; Carbohydrate 17g (Dietary Fiber 1g); Protein 26g

MAKE IT A MEAL

Enjoy this low-fat favorite with a cool cucumber salad. Top cucumber slices with chopped red onion, a sprinkling of toasted sesame seeds and a splash of red wine vinegar.

Lemon-Ginger Chicken

4 SERVINGS PREP TIME: **15 MINUTES** START TO FINISH: **25 MINUTES**

4 boneless, skinless chicken breast halves (about 1¼ pounds)

½ cup Original Bisquick®

¼ cup plain bread crumbs

1 tablespoon grated lemon peel

½ teaspoon grated gingerroot

½ cup water

3 tablespoons vegetable oil

Lemon Sauce (right)

Lemon slices, if desired

1. Flatten each chicken breast half to about ¼-inch thickness between sheets of plastic wrap or waxed paper.

2. Mix Bisquick, bread crumbs, lemon peel and gingerroot. Pour water into shallow glass or plastic bowl. Dip chicken into water, then coat with Bisquick mixture.

3. Heat oil in 12-inch nonstick skillet over medium heat. Cook chicken in oil 8 to 10 minutes, turning once, until juice is no longer pink when centers of thickest pieces are cut.

4. While chicken is cooking, make Lemon Sauce. Pour over cooked chicken. Garnish with lemon slices if desired.

LEMON SAUCE

¼ cup lemon juice

¼ cup water

3 tablespoons sugar

1 tablespoon cornstarch

¼ teaspoon grated gingerroot

1 drop yellow food color, if desired

Mix all ingredients in 1-quart saucepan. Heat over medium heat, stirring occasionally, until thickened and bubbly.

1 serving: Calories 375 (Calories from Fat 155); Fat 17g (Saturated 3g); Cholesterol 75mg; Sodium 340mg; Carbohydrate 27g (Dietary Fiber 0g); Protein 29g

Betty's Tip

Flatten chicken breasts by pounding with a meat mallet, rolling pin or even the heel of your hand. Thinner chicken breasts cook more evenly and quickly, so it's good to take time to flatten them, even when you're short on time.

Feta-Topped Chicken with Bulgur

4 SERVINGS PREP TIME: **25 MINUTES** START TO FINISH: **38 MINUTES**

4 boneless, skinless chicken breast halves (about 1¼ pounds)

2 tablespoons balsamic vinaigrette dressing

1 teaspoon Italian seasoning

¼ teaspoon seasoned pepper

⅔ cup uncooked bulgur

2 cups water

1 large roma (plum) tomato, cut into 8 slices

¼ cup crumbled feta cheese (1 ounce)

Betty's Tip

Bulgur wheat is a quick-cooking whole grain that's becoming more popular. Rather than just cooking it in water, you can cook it in chicken or vegetable broth for extra flavor.

1. Set oven control to broil. Brush both sides of chicken breasts with dressing. Sprinkle both sides with Italian seasoning and seasoned pepper. Place on rack in broiler pan.

2. Broil with tops 4 inches from heat about 10 minutes, turning once, until juice is no longer pink when centers of thickest pieces are cut.

3. Meanwhile, cook bulgur in water as directed on package, omitting salt.

4. Top chicken with tomato and cheese. Broil 2 to 3 minutes longer or until cheese is lightly browned. Serve with bulgur.

1 serving: Calories 250 (Calories from Fat 90); Fat 10g (Saturated 3g); Cholesterol 90mg; Sodium 360mg; Carbohydrate 7g (Dietary Fiber 2g); Protein 33g

Jamaican Jerk Chicken

6 SERVINGS PREP TIME: **10 MINUTES** START TO FINISH: **35 MINUTES**

6 small boneless, skinless chicken breast halves (about 1½ pounds)

2 tablespoons freeze-dried chives

1 tablespoon instant minced onion

1 tablespoon instant minced garlic

1 teaspoon crushed red pepper

1 teaspoon ground coriander

1 teaspoon ground ginger

1 medium pineapple (3 pounds), peeled and cut into 6 slices

Hot cooked rice, if desired

Betty's Tip

This easy-to-fix recipe relies on the Jamaican cooking technique of "jerking"—rubbing a food with a dry mixture of herbs and spices—to boost flavor without adding fat and calories.

1. Heat oven to 425°. Spray rectangular pan, 13 × 9 × 2 inches, with cooking spray. Remove fat from chicken.

2. Place chives, onion flakes, garlic flakes, red pepper, coriander and ginger in blender or food processor. Cover and blend on high speed about 30 seconds or until blended. Rub both sides of chicken breast halves with chive mixture.

3. Place pineapple slices in pan. Place 1 chicken breast half on each pineapple slice. Bake uncovered about 25 minutes or until juice of chicken is no longer pink when centers of thickest pieces are cut. Serve chicken and pineapple over rice if desired.

1 serving: Calories 190 (Calories from Fat 35); Fat 4g (Saturated 1g); Cholesterol 70mg; Sodium 65mg; Carbohydrate 16g (Dietary Fiber 2g); Protein 25g

Spinach and Chicken Sauté

6 SERVINGS PREP TIME: **10 MINUTES** START TO FINISH: **26 MINUTES**

6 small boneless, skinless chicken breast halves (about 1½ pounds)

1 cup fat-free (skim) milk

½ cup chicken broth

1 medium onion, chopped (½ cup)

1 bag (10 ounces) washed fresh spinach, chopped

¼ teaspoon salt

¼ teaspoon pepper

¼ teaspoon ground nutmeg

1. Remove fat from chicken. Spray 12-inch nonstick skillet with cooking spray and heat skillet over medium heat. Cook chicken in skillet 2 minutes on each side, then reduce heat to medium-low. Stir in milk, broth and onion. Cook about 5 minutes, turning chicken occasionally, until onion is tender.

2. Stir in spinach. Cook 3 to 4 minutes, stirring occasionally, until spinach is completely wilted and juice of chicken is no longer pink when centers of thickest pieces are cut. Remove chicken from skillet; keep warm.

3. Increase heat to medium. Cook spinach mixture about 3 minutes or until liquid has almost evaporated. Stir in salt, pepper and nutmeg. Serve chicken on spinach.

1 serving: Calories 165 (Calories from Fat 35); Fat 4g (Saturated 2g); Cholesterol 70mg; Sodium 300mg; Carbohydrate 5g (Dietary Fiber 1g); Protein 28g

Honey-Spiced Chicken with Carrots and Grapes

4 SERVINGS PREP TIME: **10 MINUTES** START TO FINISH: **26 MINUTES**

4 boneless, skinless chicken breast halves (about 1 pound)

3 medium carrots, cut into julienne strips (2 cups)

2 cups seedless red grapes, cut in half

⅓ cup orange juice

1 tablespoon honey

1 tablespoon balsamic or red wine vinegar

¼ teaspoon ground cinnamon

¼ teaspoon ground nutmeg

Hot cooked rice, if desired

Chopped fresh parsley, if desired

Betty's Tip

If your family prefers dark meat, make this recipe with boneless chicken thighs.

1. Remove fat from chicken. Place chicken and remaining ingredients except rice and parsley in 10-inch nonstick skillet. Heat to boiling; reduce heat. Cover and simmer about 10 minutes, stirring occasionally, until juice of chicken is no longer pink when centers of thickest pieces are cut.

2. Remove chicken and keep warm. Heat sauce in skillet to boiling and reduce heat. Simmer uncovered 2 minutes, stirring occasionally. Serve chicken on rice if desired and pour sauce over chicken. Sprinkle with parsley if desired.

1 serving: Calories 235 (Calories from Fat 35); Fat 4g (Saturated 2g); Cholesterol 70mg; Sodium 80mg; Carbohydrate 26g (Dietary Fiber 2g); Protein 26g

Cajun Chicken

4 SERVINGS PREP TIME: **10 MINUTES** START TO FINISH: **20 MINUTES**

4 boneless, skinless chicken breast halves (about 1¼ pounds)

1½ cups cornflakes cereal, crushed (½ cup)

½ cup Original Bisquick®

2 teaspoons Cajun seasoning

½ cup water

2 tablespoons margarine or butter

Betty's Tip

For a southern-style chicken sandwich, serve in toasted sesame buns with barbecue sauce, lettuce, red onion and tomato slices.

1. Flatten each chicken breast half to about ¼-inch thickness between sheets of plastic wrap or waxed paper.

2. Mix cereal, Bisquick and Cajun seasoning. Dip chicken into water, then coat with cereal mixture.

3. Melt margarine in 12-inch nonstick skillet over medium heat. Cook chicken in margarine 8 to 10 minutes, turning once, until juice is no longer pink when centers of thickest pieces are cut.

1 serving: Calories 275 (Calories from Fat 90); Fat 10g (Saturated 2g); Cholesterol 75mg; Sodium 450mg; Carbohydrate 18g (Dietary Fiber 1g); Protein 28g

Wild Mushroom Herbed Chicken

6 SERVINGS PREP TIME: **10 MINUTES** START TO FINISH: **30 MINUTES**

6 small boneless, skinless chicken breast halves (about 1½ pounds)

¾ pound assorted wild mushrooms (such as oyster, shiitake and chanterelle), coarsely chopped (5 cups)

1 medium leek, sliced (2 cups)

3 cloves garlic, finely chopped

1 can (14½ ounces) chicken broth

½ cup dry white wine or chicken broth

2 tablespoons cornstarch

½ teaspoon dried thyme leaves

Hot cooked couscous, if desired

Betty's Tip

Wild mushrooms have a fuller and more robust flavor than the white cultivated mushrooms you find most often in the store. Look for varieties such as oyster, shiitake or chanterelle.

1. Remove fat from chicken. Spray 12-inch nonstick skillet with cooking spray and heat over medium heat. Cook chicken in skillet about 12 minutes, turning once, until juice is no longer pink when centers of thickest pieces are cut. Remove chicken from skillet; keep warm.

2. Cook mushrooms, leek and garlic in same skillet about 3 minutes, stirring frequently, until leek is tender. Mix broth, wine, cornstarch and thyme and stir into mushroom mixture. Heat to boiling, stirring occasionally. Boil and stir about 1 minute or until slightly thickened.

3. Add chicken and heat through. Serve chicken on couscous if desired.

1 serving: Calories 170 (Calories from Fat 35); Fat 4g (Saturated 1g); Cholesterol 70mg; Sodium 360mg; Carbohydrate 7g (Dietary Fiber 1g); Protein 28g

MAKE IT A MEAL

Steamed green beans are nice on the side.

Thai Chicken with Spicy Peanut Sauce

4 SERVINGS PREP TIME: **10 MINUTES** START TO FINISH: **40 MINUTES**

3 tablespoons margarine or butter

1 cup Original Bisquick®

1½ teaspoons curry powder

1½ teaspoons garlic powder

1 teaspoon ground ginger

4 boneless, skinless chicken breast halves (about 1¼ pounds)

⅓ cup milk

Spicy Peanut Sauce (right)

2 tablespoons cocktail peanuts, finely chopped

1. Heat oven to 425°. Melt margarine in rectangular baking dish, 13 × 9 × 2 inches, in oven.

2. Mix Bisquick, curry powder, garlic powder and ginger. Dip chicken into milk, then coat with Bisquick mixture. Place in dish.

3. Bake uncovered 20 minutes; turn chicken. Bake about 10 minutes longer or until juice of chicken is no longer pink when centers of thickest pieces are cut. While chicken is baking, make Spicy Peanut Sauce. Serve sauce over chicken. Sprinkle with peanuts.

SPICY PEANUT SAUCE

½ cup plain yogurt

¼ cup creamy peanut butter

½ cup milk

1 tablespoon soy sauce

⅛ teaspoon ground red pepper (cayenne)

Mix all ingredients in 10-inch nonstick skillet. Cook over medium heat 3 to 4 minutes, stirring occasionally, until mixture begins to thicken.

1 serving: Calories 510 (Calories from Fat 260); Fat 29g (Saturated 7g); Cholesterol 0mg; Sodium 950mg; Carbohydrate 27g (Dietary Fiber 2g); Protein 37g

MAKE IT A MEAL

Serve this spicy chicken over hot cooked jasmine rice with steamed carrots and broccoli or broccolini, a new kind of broccoli that has sparse flowerets.

Crunchy Garlic Chicken

6 SERVINGS PREP TIME: **15 MINUTES** START TO FINISH: **40 MINUTES**

6 small boneless, skinless chicken breast halves (about 1½ pounds)

3 tablespoons margarine, melted

1 tablespoon fat-free (skim) milk

1 tablespoon chopped fresh chives or parsley

½ teaspoon salt

½ teaspoon garlic powder

2 cups cornflakes cereal, crushed (1 cup)

3 tablespoons chopped fresh parsley

½ teaspoon paprika

Cooking spray

1. Heat oven to 425°. Spray rectangular pan, 13 × 9 × 2 inches, with cooking spray. Remove fat from chicken. Mix margarine, milk, chives, salt and garlic powder. Mix cornflakes, parsley and paprika in separate bowl.

2. Dip chicken into margarine mixture, then coat lightly and evenly with cornflakes mixture. Place in pan. Spray chicken with cooking spray. Bake uncovered 20 to 25 minutes or until juice is no longer pink when centers of thickest pieces are cut.

1 serving: Calories 220 (Calories from Fat 80); Fat 9g (Saturated 3g); Cholesterol 70mg; Sodium 430mg; Carbohydrate 9g (Dietary Fiber 0g); Protein 26g

MAKE IT A MEAL
Fresh Melon Salad

6 SERVINGS PREP TIME: **10 MINUTES** START TO FINISH: **10 MINUTES**

2 cups watermelon balls or cubes

2 mangoes or papayas, peeled, seeded and sliced

½ honeydew melon, peeled, seeded and thinly sliced

¾ cup seedless red grapes

Lettuce leaves

Honey-Lime Dressing (right)

Arrange fruits on lettuce leaves. Drizzle with Honey-Lime Dressing.

HONEY-LIME DRESSING

¼ cup vegetable oil

¼ teaspoon grated lime peel

2 tablespoons lime juice

1 tablespoon honey

Shake all ingredients in tightly covered container.

1 serving: Calories 208 (Calories from Fat 85); Fat 10g (Saturated 1g); Cholesterol 0mg; Sodium 22mg; Carbohydrate 33g (Dietary Fiber 3g); Protein 2g

Chicken Picadillo

4 SERVINGS PREP TIME: **15 MINUTES** START TO FINISH: **33 MINUTES**

4 boneless, skinless chicken breast halves (about 1 pound)

1 can (14½ ounces) Mexican-style stewed tomatoes, undrained

1 medium unpeeled tart cooking apple, coarsely chopped (1 cup)

⅓ cup orange juice

1 to 2 jalapeño chilies, seeded and finely chopped

2 tablespoons raisins

2 tablespoons white vinegar

3 tablespoons orange juice

2 teaspoons cornstarch

Hot cooked rice, if desired

Slivered almonds, toasted, if desired

1. Remove fat from chicken. Cut chicken into 2-inch pieces. Drain tomatoes, reserving liquid. Cut up tomatoes.

2. Heat tomatoes, tomato liquid, apple, ⅓ cup orange juice, the chilies, raisins and vinegar to boiling in 12-inch nonstick skillet; reduce heat. Stir in chicken. Cover and simmer about 10 minutes or until juice of chicken is no longer pink when centers of thickest pieces are cut.

3. Mix 3 tablespoons orange juice and the cornstarch. Stir into chicken mixture. Heat to boiling, stirring constantly. Boil and stir 1 minute. Serve chicken mixture on rice if desired. Sprinkle with almonds if desired.

1 serving: Calories 220 (Calories from Fat 35); Fat 4g (Saturated 1g); Cholesterol 70mg; Sodium 350mg; Carbohydrate 22g (Dietary Fiber 2g); Protein 26g

Spicy Mexican Skillet Chicken

4 SERVINGS PREP TIME: **10 MINUTES** START TO FINISH: **25 MINUTES**

1 to 2 teaspoons chili powder

¼ teaspoon salt

¼ teaspoon pepper

4 boneless, skinless chicken breast halves (about 1 pound)

1 tablespoon vegetable oil

1 can (15 ounces) black beans, rinsed and drained

1 cup frozen whole kernel corn

⅓ cup thick-and-chunky salsa

Chopped fresh cilantro, if desired

1. Mix chili powder, salt and pepper. Sprinkle evenly over both sides of chicken breast halves.

2. Heat oil in 10-inch skillet over medium heat. Cook chicken in oil 8 to 10 minutes, turning once, until juice is no longer pink when centers of thickest pieces are cut.

3. Stir in beans, corn and salsa. Heat to boiling; reduce heat. Cover and simmer 3 to 5 minutes or until vegetables are hot. Sprinkle with cilantro if desired.

1 serving: Calories 258 (Calories from Fat 48); Fat 6g (Saturated 1g); Cholesterol 66mg; Sodium 649mg; Carbohydrate 23g (Dietary Fiber 5g); Protein 32g

Betty's Tips

Serve with lime wedges to squeeze on top.

Black beans can be hard to find. Sometimes they're shelved with other canned beans; they're often found with Mexican ingredients. If you can't find them in either location, kidney or pinto beans can be used instead.

MAKE IT A MEAL

Hot corn bread with a drizzle of honey is all that's needed to make this meal complete.

Quick Chicken
with Olives and Tomatoes

6 SERVINGS PREP TIME: **10 MINUTES** START TO FINISH: **35 MINUTES**

2 tablespoons margarine or butter

2 cloves garlic, crushed

1 small onion, chopped (about ¼ cup)

6 small boneless, skinless chicken breast
halves (about 1½ pounds)

½ cup red wine vinegar

2 teaspoons chopped fresh or ½ teaspoon
dried thyme leaves

½ teaspoon salt

¼ teaspoon pepper

2 large tomatoes, chopped (about 2 cups)

1 can (2¼ ounces) sliced ripe olives, drained

1. Heat margarine in 10-inch skillet over
medium-high heat until melted. Cook garlic,
onion and chicken in margarine until
chicken is brown on both sides.

2. Stir in remaining ingredients; reduce heat.
Cook 10 to 15 minutes or until juice of
chicken is no longer pink when centers of
thickest pieces are cut.

1 serving: Calories 188 (Calories from Fat 58); Fat 6g
(Saturated 1g); Cholesterol 66mg; Sodium 408mg;
Carbohydrate 5g (Dietary Fiber 1g); Protein 27g

MAKE IT A MEAL

Serve the chicken on a bed of hot buttered orzo.

Chicken Linguine Alfredo

6 SERVINGS PREP TIME: **25 MINUTES** START TO FINISH: **40 MINUTES**

ALFREDO SAUCE

2 teaspoons butter or margarine

2 tablespoons finely chopped shallot

1 clove garlic, crushed

1 pint fat-free half-and-half (2 cups)

3 tablespoons all-purpose flour

½ cup reduced-fat sour cream

½ cup grated Parmesan cheese

½ teaspoon salt

⅛ teaspoon white pepper

LINGUINE MIXTURE

8 ounces uncooked linguine

1¼ pounds cut-up boneless chicken breast strips for stir-fry

1 jar (7 ounces) roasted red bell peppers, drained and thinly sliced

⅓ cup shredded Parmesan cheese

2 tablespoons chopped fresh parsley

1. Melt butter in 2-quart saucepan over medium heat. Add shallot and garlic. Cook and stir 1 minute. Remove garlic from saucepan and discard. In medium bowl, beat half-and-half and flour with wire whisk; add to saucepan. Heat to boiling, stirring frequently. Beat in sour cream with wire whisk. Reduce heat to low and cook 1 to 2 minutes or until heated. Remove from heat and stir in ½ cup Parmesan cheese, salt and white pepper.

2. Cook linguine in 4-quart Dutch oven as directed on package. Drain and rinse with hot water. Return to Dutch oven to keep warm.

3. Meanwhile, spray 12-inch nonstick skillet with cooking spray and heat over medium-high heat. Add chicken and cook about 5 minutes, stirring frequently, until no longer pink in center.

4. Add chicken, bell peppers and Alfredo sauce to linguine; stir to mix. Cook over low heat until thoroughly heated. Garnish with ⅓ cup Parmesan cheese and parsley.

1 serving: Calories 430 (Calories from Fat 110); Fat 13g (Saturated 6g); Cholesterol 80mg; Sodium 760mg; Carbohydrate 44g (Dietary Fiber 3g); Protein 35g

Spring Chicken Pasta

6 SERVINGS PREP TIME: **20 MINUTES** START TO FINISH: **30 MINUTES**

1½ pounds boneless, skinless chicken breasts

8 ounces uncooked spaghetti

1 pound asparagus, cut into 2-inch pieces

8 sun-dried tomato halves (not in oil), chopped

2 cloves garlic, finely chopped

1 large yellow bell pepper, chopped (1½ cups)

¾ cup chopped red onion

2 cups chicken broth

¾ cup fat-free ricotta cheese

⅓ cup chopped fresh basil leaves

2 tablespoons reduced-fat sour cream

½ teaspoon salt

¼ teaspoon pepper

1. Remove fat from chicken. Cut chicken into ½-inch strips. Cook and drain spaghetti as directed on package, except omit salt.

2. While pasta is cooking, cook asparagus, tomatoes, garlic, bell pepper, onion and broth in 3-quart saucepan over medium heat 5 minutes. Stir in chicken. Cook 2 to 3 minutes, stirring constantly, until asparagus is crisp-tender and chicken is no longer pink in center.

3. Stir in spaghetti and remaining ingredients. Toss about 30 seconds or until heated through.

1 serving: Calories 355 (Calories from Fat 55); Fat 6g (Saturated 2g); Cholesterol 70mg; Sodium 680mg; Carbohydrate 40g (Dietary Fiber 3g); Protein 38g

Betty's Tip

Ricotta is a fresh, unaged cheese that is just a bit grainy but smoother than cottage cheese. It is very moist, with a slightly sweet flavor, and is widely used in both main dishes and desserts.

Quick Italian Chicken Sandwich

4 SERVINGS PREP TIME: **10 MINUTES** START TO FINISH: **20 MINUTES**

4 boneless, skinless chicken breast halves (about 1¼ pounds)

½ cup Original Bisquick®

½ cup grated Parmesan cheese

2 teaspoons Italian seasoning

½ cup water

2 tablespoons butter or margarine

4 hoagie buns, split

Lettuce leaves, if desired

4 slices (1 ounce each) fresh mozzarella cheese

1 cup tomato pasta or marinara sauce, heated

1. Flatten each chicken breast half to about ¼-inch thickness between sheets of plastic wrap or waxed paper.

2. Mix Bisquick, Parmesan cheese and Italian seasoning. Dip chicken into water, then coat with Bisquick mixture.

3. Melt butter in 12-inch nonstick skillet over medium heat. Cook chicken in butter 8 to 10 minutes, turning once, until no longer pink when centers of thickest pieces are cut. Fill buns with chicken, lettuce (if desired), mozzarella cheese and pasta sauce.

1 sandwich: Calories 590 (Calories from Fat 190); Fat 21g (Saturated 10g); Cholesterol 110mg; Sodium 1,350mg; Carbohydrate 55g (Dietary Fiber 3g); Protein 45g

Betty's Tip

Dip chicken into red wine vinegar instead of the water for a zesty Italian taste. If you don't have Italian seasoning, you can use ½ teaspoon each of dried basil, marjoram, oregano and thyme leaves.

Fruity Chicken Salad with Spring Greens and Pecans

4 SERVINGS PREP TIME: **20 MINUTES** START TO FINISH: **30 MINUTES**

2 boneless, skinless chicken breast halves (about ½ pound)

1 cup cut-up red grapes

2 medium stalks celery, thinly sliced (1 cup)

½ cup dried cherries

¼ cup finely chopped onion

¾ cup fat-free honey-mustard dressing or other fat-free dressing

8 cups mixed spring greens

¼ cup chopped pecans, toasted

Betty's Tips

In this tasty salad, you can try other types of dried fruits, such as dried cranberries, cut-up dried apricots or golden raisins.

To toast nuts, spread in ungreased shallow pan and bake at 350° for 6 to 10 minutes, stirring occasionally, until light brown and aromatic.

1. Brush grill rack with vegetable oil. Heat coals or gas grill. Place chicken on grill and cover. Cook over medium heat 7 to 10 minutes, turning halfway through cooking, until juice is no longer pink when centers of thickest pieces are cut. Cool and cut into bite-size pieces.

2. Mix chicken, grapes, celery, cherries, onion and ½ cup of the dressing in large bowl.

3. Divide greens among 4 plates. Top with chicken mixture and sprinkle with pecans. Drizzle each salad with 1 tablespoon dressing.

1 serving: Calories 300 (Calories from Fat 70); Fat 7g (Saturated 1g); Cholesterol 35mg; Sodium 600mg; Carbohydrate 42g (Dietary Fiber 6g); Protein 16g

Tropical Chicken Salad

4 SERVINGS PREP TIME: **25 MINUTES** START TO FINISH: **35 MINUTES**

1¼ pounds boneless, skinless chicken breasts, cut into ½-inch strips

1 tablespoon blackened seasoning blend

1 tablespoon canola oil

1 bag (5 ounces) mixed baby salad greens (4 cups)

2 medium mangoes, seeds removed, peeled and diced (2 cups)

½ medium red onion, sliced (¾ cup)

1 small red bell pepper, chopped (½ cup)

⅔ cup fat-free raspberry vinaigrette

1. Place chicken in heavy-duty resealable plastic food-storage bag. Sprinkle seasoning blend over chicken. Seal bag and shake until chicken is evenly coated.

2. Heat oil in 10-inch nonstick skillet over medium-high heat. Cook chicken in oil 7 to 10 minutes, stirring frequently, until no longer pink in center. Remove chicken from skillet and drain on paper towels.

3. Toss salad greens, mangoes, onion and bell pepper in large bowl. Divide among 4 plates. Top with chicken. Drizzle with vinaigrette.

1 serving: Calories 340 (Calories from Fat 80); Fat 8g (Saturated 1.5g); Cholesterol 85mg; Sodium 590mg; Carbohydrate 34g (Dietary Fiber 4g); Protein 33g

Slow-Cooker Chicken-Barley Stew

6 SERVINGS PREP TIME: **15 MINUTES** START TO FINISH: **8 HOURS 30 MINUTES**

3 large carrots, sliced (2 cups)

2 medium stalks celery, sliced (1 cup)

1 large onion, chopped (1 cup)

2 skinless, bone-in chicken breast halves (about 1¼ pounds)

5 cups water

¾ cup uncooked medium pearled barley

2 teaspoons chicken bouillon granules

½ teaspoon salt

¼ teaspoon pepper

1 can (14½ ounces) diced tomatoes, undrained

2 tablespoons chopped fresh parsley

1 teaspoon dried thyme leaves

1. Place carrots, celery and onion in 4- to 5-quart slow cooker. Place chicken breasts on vegetables. Add remaining ingredients except parsley and thyme.

2. Cover and cook on low heat setting 8 to 9 hours.

3. Remove chicken from cooker and place on cutting board. Remove meat from bones and chop into ½- to 1-inch pieces; discard bones.

4. Stir chicken, parsley and thyme into stew. Increase heat setting to high. Cover and cook 10 to 15 minutes longer or until chicken is thoroughly heated.

1 serving: Calories 220 (Calories from Fat 25); Fat 3g (Saturated 0.5g); Cholesterol 40mg; Sodium 650mg; Carbohydrate 30g (Dietary Fiber 7g); Protein 19g

Crispy Basil Chicken

6 SERVINGS PREP TIME: **10 MINUTES** START TO FINISH: **30 MINUTES**

⅓ cup cholesterol-free egg product

2 tablespoons chicken broth

1 tablespoon Dijon mustard

1 clove garlic, finely chopped

1½ cups dry bread crumbs

1 tablespoon dried basil leaves

1 teaspoon paprika

¼ teaspoon white pepper

12 boneless, skinless chicken thighs
   (about 1½ pounds)

1. Heat oven to 400°. Spray shallow roasting pan with cooking spray.

2. Mix egg product, broth, mustard and garlic in small bowl. Mix bread crumbs, basil, paprika and white pepper in heavy-duty resealable plastic food-storage bag.

3. Dip chicken into egg mixture, then shake in bag to coat with crumb mixture. Place in pan. Bake uncovered about 20 minutes or until juice is no longer pink when centers of thickest pieces are cut.

1 serving: Calories 282 (Calories from Fat 62); Fat 7g (Saturated 2g); Cholesterol 115mg; Sodium 419mg; Carbohydrate 21g (Dietary Fiber 2g); Protein 32g

MAKE IT A MEAL

For a quick salad, top shredded lettuce with a scoop of guacamole and sprinkle with chopped tomato.

Tequila Chicken

4 SERVINGS PREP TIME: **10 MINUTES** START TO FINISH: **33 MINUTES**

8 boneless, skinless chicken thighs (about 1⅓ pounds)

1 medium onion, cut into 8 wedges and separated

1 can (15 ounces) tomato sauce

¼ cup tequila or chicken broth

2 tablespoons molasses

1 tablespoon lime juice

1 teaspoon crushed red pepper

½ teaspoon ground cumin

Hot cooked brown rice, if desired

Lime wedges, if desired

1. Remove fat from chicken. Spray 12-inch nonstick skillet with cooking spray and heat over medium heat. Cook chicken in skillet about 5 minutes, turning once, until brown. Remove chicken from skillet.

2. Add remaining ingredients except rice and lime wedges to skillet. Heat to boiling; reduce heat. Return chicken to skillet. Cover and simmer about 10 minutes or until juice of chicken is no longer pink when centers of thickest pieces are cut. Uncover and simmer 3 minutes longer.

3. Serve chicken on rice if desired. Pour sauce over chicken. Serve with lime wedges if desired.

1 serving: Calories 305 (Calories from Fat 110); Fat 12g (Saturated 4g); Cholesterol 95mg; Sodium 730mg; Carbohydrate 18g (Dietary Fiber 2g); Protein 33g

MAKE IT A MEAL

Serve this Tex-Mex-style barbecued chicken over whole wheat fettuccine if you prefer.

Chicken with Basil-Seasoned Vegetables

4 SERVINGS PREP TIME: **10 MINUTES** START TO FINISH: **39 MINUTES**

2 pounds chicken drumsticks

1 can (14½ ounces) chicken broth

1 can (5½ ounces) spicy eight-vegetable juice

1½ teaspoons dried basil leaves

½ teaspoon cracked black pepper

1 bag (1 pound) frozen green beans, potatoes, onions and red peppers, thawed

2 tablespoons cornstarch

Hot cooked noodles, if desired

1. Spray 12-inch nonstick skillet with cooking spray and heat over medium heat. Cook chicken in skillet about 10 minutes, turning occasionally, until brown on all sides. Remove chicken from skillet; keep warm.

2. Reserve 2 tablespoons of the broth. Add remaining broth, the vegetable juice, basil and pepper to skillet. Heat to boiling; reduce heat. Arrange chicken in broth mixture. Add vegetables. Cover and simmer about 15 minutes, stirring occasionally, until juice of chicken is no longer pink when centers of thickest pieces are cut. Remove chicken and keep warm.

3. Mix reserved 2 tablespoons broth and the cornstarch. Stir into vegetable mixture. Heat to boiling, stirring constantly. Boil and stir 1 minute. Serve over chicken and noodles if desired.

1 serving: Calories 300 (Calories from Fat 110);
Fat 12g (Saturated 4g); Cholesterol 90mg;
Sodium 630mg; Carbohydrate 17g (Dietary Fiber 3g);
Protein 34g

Chili-Coated Chicken Drummies

4 SERVINGS PREP TIME: **10 MINUTES** START TO FINISH: **29 MINUTES**

½ cup Original Bisquick®

2 tablespoons yellow cornmeal

2 teaspoons chili powder

1 teaspoon paprika

½ teaspoon salt

⅛ teaspoon pepper

8 chicken drumsticks, thighs or wings (about 2 pounds)

1. Mix all ingredients except chicken in 2-quart resealable plastic food-storage bag.

2. Shake 2 pieces of chicken at a time in bag until coated. Arrange chicken, skin sides up and thickest parts to outside edge, in ungreased microwavable pie plate, 9 × 1¼ inches.

3. Cover with waxed paper. Microwave on High 10 minutes. Rotate pie plate ½ turn. Microwave 6 to 9 minutes longer or until juice is no longer pink when centers of thickest pieces are cut.

1 serving: Calories 275 (Calories from Fat 115); Fat 13g (Saturated 4g); Cholesterol 85mg; Sodium 600mg; Carbohydrate 13g (Dietary Fiber 1g); Protein 30g

Betty's Tip

Using all of the same kind of chicken pieces helps to cook the chicken evenly, which is especially important for microwave cooking. To check if it's fully cooked through, cut into the chicken with a sharp knife. The juices should be clear, not pink.

Slow-Cooker Southwest Chicken Soup

6 SERVINGS PREP TIME: **15 MINUTES** START TO FINISH: **7 HOURS 45 MINUTES**

1 pound boneless, skinless chicken thighs, cut into 1-inch pieces

2 medium dark-orange sweet potatoes, peeled and cut into 1-inch pieces (2 cups)

1 large onion, chopped (1 cup)

2 cans (14½ ounces each) diced tomatoes and green chilies, undrained

1 can (14 ounces) reduced-sodium chicken broth

1 teaspoon dried oregano leaves

½ teaspoon ground cumin

1 cup frozen whole kernel corn

½ cup chopped green bell pepper

8 yellow or blue corn tortillas (5 or 6 inches in diameter)

2 tablespoons chopped fresh cilantro

1. Mix chicken, sweet potatoes, onion, tomatoes, broth, oregano and cumin in 3½- to 4-quart slow cooker.

2. Cover and cook on low heat setting 7 to 8 hours.

3. Stir corn and bell pepper into soup. Increase heat setting to high. Cover and cook about 30 minutes longer.

4. Meanwhile, heat oven to 450°. Spray 2 cookie sheets with cooking spray. Cut each tortilla into strips and place in single layer on cookie sheets. Bake about 6 minutes or until crisp but not brown; cool. Spoon soup into bowls. Top with tortilla strips. Sprinkle with cilantro.

1 serving: Calories 300 (Calories from Fat 60); Fat 7g (Saturated 2g); Cholesterol 45mg; Sodium 660mg; Carbohydrate 37g (Dietary Fiber 7g); Protein 23g

Sweet-and-Sour Chicken Crepes

4 SERVINGS (2 CREPES EACH) PREP TIME: **20 MINUTES** START TO FINISH: **25 MINUTES**

Crepes (right)

2 cups frozen stir-fry bell peppers and onions (from 1-pound bag), thawed and drained

1 cup cut-up cooked chicken

1 can (8 ounces) pineapple tidbits or chunks, drained

2/3 cup sweet-and-sour sauce

1. Make Crepes.

2. Heat vegetables, chicken, pineapple and 1/3 cup of the sweet-and-sour sauce in 2-quart saucepan over medium-high heat, stirring constantly, until hot.

3. Spoon about 2 tablespoons filling onto each crepe. Roll up and carefully place seam side down. Heat remaining 1/3 cup sweet-and-sour sauce until hot. Serve over crepes.

SPEED SUPPER

Make the crepes ahead of time. Stack crepes with waxed paper between them, place them in a plastic bag (so they won't dry out) and refrigerate. At suppertime, make the filling and quickly reheat the crepes in the microwave on High for 30 seconds. Assemble and serve.

CREPES

1 cup Original Bisquick®

3/4 cup milk

1 teaspoon soy sauce

1 egg

1. Stir all ingredients until blended. Lightly spray 6- or 7-inch skillet with cooking spray and heat over medium-high heat.

2. For each crepe, pour 2 tablespoons batter into hot skillet. Rotate skillet until batter covers bottom. Cook until golden brown. Gently loosen edge with metal spatula. Turn and cook other side until golden brown.

3. Stack crepes as you remove them from skillet, placing waxed paper between them. Keep crepes covered to prevent them from drying out.

1 serving: Calories 325 (Calories from Fat 90); Fat 10g (Saturated 3g); Cholesterol 85mg; Sodium 730mg; Carbohydrate 43g (Dietary Fiber 3g); Protein 16g

Creamy Chicken and Corn with Fettuccine

4 SERVINGS PREP TIME: **10 MINUTES** START TO FINISH: **15 MINUTES**

8 ounces uncooked fettuccine or linguine

1 package (10 ounces) frozen whole kernel corn, thawed

6 medium green onions, sliced (6 tablespoons)

1 tub (8 ounces) soft reduced-fat cream cheese with roasted garlic

1/3 cup fat-free (skim) milk

1 1/2 cups cut-up cooked chicken or turkey

1 jar (2 ounces) diced pimientos, drained

1/4 teaspoon pepper

Chopped fresh parsley, if desired

1. Cook and drain fettuccine as directed on package.

2. While pasta is cooking, spray 12-inch non-stick skillet with cooking spray and heat over medium heat. Cook corn and onions in skillet about 4 minutes, stirring frequently, until corn is crisp-tender.

3. Stir cream cheese and milk into corn mixture until blended. Stir in chicken, pimientos and pepper; heat through.

4. Stir fettuccine into sauce; heat through. Sprinkle with parsley if desired.

1 serving: Calories 465 (Calories from Fat 135); Fat 15g (Saturated 8g); Cholesterol 120mg; Sodium 340mg; Carbohydrate 57g (Dietary Fiber 4g); Protein 30g

MAKE IT A MEAL

Serve store-bought ice cream sandwiches as an impromptu dessert by topping with fresh fruit or ice cream toppings and whipped cream.

Cheesy Chicken Casserole

6 SERVINGS PREP TIME: **10 MINUTES** START TO FINISH: **32 MINUTES**

2 cups cut-up cooked chicken

1 jar (16 ounces) Cheddar cheese pasta sauce

1 bag (1 pound) frozen broccoli, carrots and cauliflower, thawed and drained

1¼ cups Original Bisquick®

¼ cup grated Parmesan cheese

¼ cup firm butter or margarine

1 egg, slightly beaten

Betty's Tip

A 16-ounce jar of purchased Alfredo pasta sauce can be used in place of the Cheddar cheese sauce for a change of flavor.

1. Heat oven to 400°. Mix chicken, pasta sauce and vegetables. Pour into ungreased square pan, $9 \times 9 \times 2$ inches.

2. Mix Bisquick and Parmesan cheese. Cut in butter using pastry blender or crisscrossing 2 knives until mixture looks like fine crumbs. Stir in egg. Sprinkle over chicken mixture.

3. Bake uncovered 20 to 22 minutes or until topping is light golden brown.

1 serving: Calories 490 (Calories from Fat 280); Fat 31g (Saturated 15g); Cholesterol 130mg; Sodium 1,030mg; Carbohydrate 25g (Dietary Fiber 3g); Protein 28g

SPEED SUPPER
Using frozen cooked chicken, thawed, or two 5-ounce cans of chunk chicken, drained, will give you a head start on this casserole.

Ultimate Chicken Pot Pie

6 SERVINGS PREP TIME: **10 MINUTES** START TO FINISH: **55 MINUTES**

1 bag (1 pound) frozen mixed vegetables

1 cup cut-up cooked chicken

1 jar (12 ounces) chicken gravy

2 cups shredded Wisconsin Cheddar cheese
(8 ounces)

1 cup Original Bisquick®

¼ cup milk

¼ cup thyme leaves

2 eggs

Betty's Tip

If you have leftover cooked vegetables, you can substitute them for the frozen vegetables.

1. Heat oven to 375°. Heat vegetables, chicken and gravy to boiling in 2-quart saucepan, stirring frequently; keep warm.

2. Stir cheese, Bisquick, milk, thyme and eggs with fork until blended. Pour chicken mixture into ungreased 2-quart casserole. Pour batter over chicken mixture.

3. Bake 35 to 40 minutes or until crust is golden brown. Let stand 5 minutes before serving.

1 serving: Calories 365 (Calories from Fat 180); Fat 20g (Saturated 10g); Cholesterol 130mg; Sodium 940mg; Carbohydrate 25g (Dietary Fiber 4g); Protein 25g

Polynesian Chicken Salad

4 SERVINGS PREP TIME: 20 MINUTES START TO FINISH: 30 MINUTES

2 teaspoons sesame seeds

2 cups water

1 package (3 ounces) chicken-flavor ramen noodle soup mix

1 can (8 ounces) pineapple tidbits, drained, 2 tablespoons juice reserved

2 tablespoons white vinegar

2 tablespoons reduced-sodium soy sauce

1 tablespoon honey

½ teaspoon ground ginger

3 cups shredded cabbage

1 cup cut-up cooked chicken

8 medium green onions, sliced (½ cup)

½ cup shredded carrot

1. Heat oven to 350°. In ungreased shallow pan, spread sesame seed. Bake 8 to 10 minutes, stirring occasionally, until golden brown and aromatic. Set aside.

2. Meanwhile, heat water to boiling in 2-quart saucepan. Break up ramen noodles before opening pouch. Remove seasoning packet from pouch. Add ramen noodles to boiling water. Cook 2 to 3 minutes, stirring occasionally, until noodles are tender; drain. Rinse in cold water to cool; drain.

3. In small bowl or 1-cup measuring cup, mix reserved pineapple juice, ½ teaspoon seasoning from ramen seasoning packet, the vinegar, soy sauce, honey and ginger. Set dressing aside.

4. In large bowl, mix noodles, pineapple, cabbage, chicken, onions and carrot. Stir in dressing and sesame seeds.

1 serving: Calories 260 (Calories from Fat 70); Fat 8g (Saturated 2g); Cholesterol 30mg; Sodium 670mg; Carbohydrate 33g (Dietary Fiber 4g); Protein 14g

Turkey Tenderloins and Mixed Sweet Peppers

4 SERVINGS PREP TIME: **10 MINUTES** START TO FINISH: **30 MINUTES**

1 pound turkey breast tenderloins

3 medium red, yellow, orange or green bell peppers, cut into ¼-inch strips

⅔ cup chicken broth

1 teaspoon dried basil leaves

¼ teaspoon salt

¼ teaspoon ground red pepper (cayenne)

3 tablespoons white wine vinegar

1 tablespoon cornstarch

Betty's Tip

Turkey tenderloins, unlike turkey breast slices, are pieces of whole muscle taken from the inside of the turkey breast. They are narrow pieces that are roughly triangular in shape, with one pointed end.

1. Spray 10-inch nonstick skillet with cooking spray and heat over medium heat. Cook turkey in skillet about 5 minutes, turning once, until brown. Remove turkey from skillet.

2. Add bell peppers to skillet. Cook over medium heat about 3 minutes, stirring frequently, until crisp-tender. Stir in broth, basil, salt and red pepper. Heat to boiling; reduce heat. Return turkey to skillet. Cover and simmer about 10 minutes, stirring occasionally, until juice of turkey is no longer pink when centers of thickest pieces are cut.

3. Remove turkey from skillet; keep warm. Push bell peppers from center of skillet. Mix vinegar and cornstarch and stir into liquid in skillet. Heat to boiling, stirring constantly. Boil and stir 1 minute. Stir peppers into sauce to coat. Cut turkey into thin slices. Serve sauce with turkey.

1 serving: Calories 155 (Calories from Fat 10); Fat 1g (Saturated 0g); Cholesterol 75mg; Sodium 370mg; Carbohydrate 9g (Dietary Fiber 1g); Protein 28g

Glazed Turkey Tenderloins

4 SERVINGS PREP TIME: **5 MINUTES** START TO FINISH: **25 MINUTES**

1 pound turkey breast tenderloins

⅓ cup orange marmalade spreadable fruit

1 teaspoon finely chopped gingerroot or
½ teaspoon ground ginger

1 teaspoon Worcestershire sauce

1. Spray 10-inch nonstick skillet with cooking spray. Cook turkey in skillet over medium heat about 5 minutes or until brown on one side; turn. Stir in remaining ingredients and reduce heat.

2. Cover and simmer about 15 minutes, stirring sauce occasionally, until sauce is thickened and juice of turkey is no longer pink when centers of thickest pieces are cut. Cut turkey into thin slices. Spoon sauce over turkey.

1 serving: Calories 175 (Calories from Fat 10); Fat 1g (Saturated 0g); Cholesterol 75mg; Sodium 65mg; Carbohydrate 16g (Dietary Fiber 1g); Protein 27g

MAKE IT A MEAL
Asparagus with Honey Mustard

2 SERVINGS PREP TIME: **3 MINUTES** START TO FINISH: **15 MINUTES**

12 to 16 spears asparagus

3 tablespoons honey

2 tablespoons Dijon mustard

4 teaspoons lemon juice

2 teaspoons olive or vegetable oil

1. Snap off tough ends of asparagus spears. Heat 1 inch water (salted if desired) to boiling in 10-inch skillet and add asparagus. Return to boiling. Cover and cook 8 to 12 minutes or until stalk ends are crisp-tender; drain.

2. Shake remaining ingredients in tightly covered container. Drizzle dressing over asparagus.

1 serving: Calories 179 (Calories from Fat 41); Fat 5g (Saturated 1g); Cholesterol 0mg; Sodium 378mg; Carbohydrate 34g (Dietary Fiber 2g); Protein 2g

Turkey Smothered with Maple Sweet Potatoes

4 SERVINGS PREP TIME: **10 MINUTES** START TO FINISH: **30 MINUTES**

1 pound turkey breast tenderloins

⅓ cup dried cranberries, dried cherries or currants

¼ cup orange juice

⅓ cup reduced-calorie maple-flavored syrup

1 tablespoon margarine

¼ teaspoon ground cinnamon

1 can (23 ounces) sweet potatoes packed in light syrup, drained

Betty's Tip

For an impressive presentation, place turkey tenderloins, overlapping slightly, around the edge of a serving platter. Omit sweet potatoes and serve with hot cooked whole wheat spaghetti. Garnish with thin twists or curls of orange peel or thin slices of orange.

1. Spray 10-inch nonstick skillet with cooking spray and heat over medium heat. Cook turkey in skillet about 5 minutes, turning once, until brown.

2. While turkey is cooking, heat cranberries, orange juice, maple syrup, margarine and cinnamon to boiling in 1-quart saucepan. Arrange sweet potatoes around turkey. Pour orange juice mixture over turkey and potatoes.

3. Cover and cook over low heat 10 minutes. Uncover and cook about 5 minutes longer or until juice of turkey is no longer pink when centers of thickest pieces are cut and sauce is slightly thickened.

1 serving: Calories 290 (Calories from Fat 35); Fat 4g (Saturated 1g); Cholesterol 75mg; Sodium 170mg; Carbohydrate 42g (Dietary Fiber 7g); Protein 28g

MAKE IT A MEAL

Serve sautéed Brussels sprouts on the side.

Greek Turkey Burgers

4 SERVINGS PREP TIME: **20 MINUTES** START TO FINISH: **30 MINUTES**

SAUCE

½ cup plain fat-free yogurt

¼ cup chopped red onion

¼ cup chopped cucumber

BURGERS

1 pound lean ground turkey

½ cup plain fat-free yogurt

1 teaspoon dried oregano leaves

½ teaspoon garlic powder

½ teaspoon salt

½ teaspoon pepper

4 whole wheat hamburger buns

1. Mix all sauce ingredients in small bowl. Refrigerate until ready to serve.

2. Set oven control to broil. Mix all burger ingredients except buns in medium bowl. Shape mixture into 4 patties, each about ½ inch thick and 5 inches in diameter. Place on rack in broiler pan.

3. Broil burgers with tops about 6 inches from heat 8 to 10 minutes, turning after 5 minutes, until no longer pink. Place burgers on buns. Serve with sauce.

1 serving: Calories 310 (Calories from Fat 70); Fat 8g (Saturated 2g); Cholesterol 75mg; Sodium 640mg; Carbohydrate 26g (Dietary Fiber 3g); Protein 33g

California-Style Turkey Patties with Corn and Tomato Relish

6 SERVINGS PREP TIME: **10 MINUTES** START TO FINISH: **22 MINUTES**

1½ pounds ground turkey breast

1 medium onion, chopped (½ cup)

1 cup soft bread crumbs (about 1½ slices bread)

½ teaspoon salt

¼ teaspoon pepper

⅓ cup chicken broth

Corn and Tomato Relish (right)

1. Mix turkey, onion, bread crumbs, salt, pepper and broth. Shape mixture into 6 patties, each about ½ inch thick.

2. Set oven control to broil. Spray broiler pan rack with cooking spray. Place patties on rack in broiler pan. Broil with tops 4 inches from heat about 12 minutes, turning once, until no longer pink in center. Serve patties with Corn and Tomato Relish.

CORN AND TOMATO RELISH

1 can (11 ounces) whole kernel corn with red and green peppers, drained

2 medium stalks celery, sliced (1 cup)

12 cherry tomatoes, cut into fourths

2 tablespoons lemon juice

Mix all ingredients.

1 serving: Calories 220 (Calories from Fat 20); Fat 2g (Saturated 1g); Cholesterol 100mg; Sodium 470mg; Carbohydrate 16g (Dietary Fiber 2g); Protein 37g

Rio Grande Turkey Soup

6 SERVINGS PREP TIME: **5 MINUTES** START TO FINISH: **20 MINUTES**

1 can (28 ounces) whole tomatoes, undrained

1 jar (16 ounces) thick-and-chunky salsa

1 can (14½ ounces) fat-free chicken broth

2 to 3 teaspoons chili powder

½ bag (16-ounce size) frozen corn, broccoli and red peppers

1 cup uncooked cavatappi pasta (3 ounces)

2 cups cut-up cooked turkey or chicken

¼ cup chopped fresh parsley

1. Heat tomatoes, salsa, broth and chili powder to boiling in 4-quart Dutch oven, breaking up tomatoes. Stir in vegetables and pasta. Heat to boiling; reduce heat.

2. Simmer uncovered about 12 minutes, stirring occasionally, until pasta and vegetables are tender. Stir in turkey and parsley and cook until hot.

1 serving: Calories 220 (Calories from Fat 45); Fat 5g (Saturated 1g); Cholesterol 40mg; Sodium 760mg; Carbohydrate 29g (Dietary Fiber 5g); Protein 20g

Turkey Wild Rice Soup

6 SERVINGS PREP TIME: **10 MINUTES** START TO FINISH: **35 MINUTES**

2 tablespoons butter or margarine

½ cup all-purpose flour

2 cans (14 ounces each) reduced-sodium chicken broth

1 package (8 ounces) 98% fat-free oven-roasted turkey breast, cubed (about 2 cups)

2 cups water

2 tablespoons instant chopped onion

1 package (6 ounces) original-flavor long-grain and wild rice mix

2 cups soy milk or fat-free (skim) milk

Betty's Tip

Wild rice is really the seed of an aquatic grass. Whatever you want to call it, the wild rice adds a delicious nutty flavor and slightly chewy texture to this quick and tasty soup.

1. Melt butter in 5-quart Dutch oven over medium heat. Stir in flour with wire whisk until well blended. Slowly stir in broth with wire whisk.

2. Stir in turkey, water, onion, rice and contents of seasoning packet. Heat to boiling over high heat, stirring occasionally. Reduce heat to medium-low. Cover and simmer about 25 minutes or until rice is tender.

3. Stir in soy milk and heat just to boiling.

1 serving: Calories 200 (Calories from Fat 50); Fat 5g (Saturated 3g); Cholesterol 45mg; Sodium 530mg; Carbohydrate 20g (Dietary Fiber 0g); Protein 18g

Caribbean Turkey Stew

5 SERVINGS PREP TIME: **20 MINUTES** START TO FINISH: **1 HOUR**

1 tablespoon canola oil

1 medium onion, coarsely chopped (½ cup)

4 cloves garlic, finely chopped

1½ pounds turkey breast tenderloins, cut into 1-inch pieces

½ teaspoon ground nutmeg

¼ teaspoon salt

¼ teaspoon pepper

1 dark-orange sweet potato, peeled and cut into 1-inch pieces (1½ cups)

2 dried bay leaves

4 small red potatoes, cut into eighths (1½ cups)

2 cups chicken broth

2 cups frozen sweet peas

1. Heat oil in 4½-quart Dutch oven over medium-high heat. Cook onion and garlic in oil 4 to 5 minutes, stirring frequently, until onion is softened.

2. Sprinkle turkey pieces with nutmeg, salt and pepper. Stir into onion mixture. Cook 5 to 6 minutes, stirring occasionally, until turkey is no longer pink in center.

3. Stir in sweet potato, bay leaves, red potatoes and broth. Heat to boiling and reduce heat to medium-low. Cover and cook 18 to 20 minutes or until potatoes are tender.

4. Stir in peas. Cover and cook 4 to 5 minutes, stirring occasionally, until peas are hot. Remove bay leaves.

1 serving: Calories 300 (Calories from Fat 45); Fat 5g (Saturated 1g); Cholesterol 90mg; Sodium 640mg; Carbohydrate 26g (Dietary Fiber 5g); Protein 38g

MAKE IT A MEAL

Serve the stew over hot basmati rice and end with fresh pineapple for dessert to complete the tropical theme.

Robust Beef and Pork Meals

Broiled Santa Fe Steaks

4 SERVINGS PREP TIME: **10 MINUTES** START TO FINISH: **21 MINUTES**

½ cup thick-and-chunky salsa

½ cup canned black beans, rinsed and drained

2 tablespoons finely chopped red onion

2 tablespoons chopped fresh cilantro

1 tablespoon lime juice

1½ teaspoons chili powder

4 boneless beef New York strip steaks (about 1½ pounds)

2 teaspoons chopped fresh or ½ teaspoon dried oregano leaves

1. Mix salsa, beans, onion, cilantro, lime juice and ½ teaspoon of the chili powder. Cover and refrigerate while preparing beef steaks.

2. Set oven control to broil. Sprinkle both sides of beef with remaining 1 teaspoon chili powder and the oregano and gently press into beef. Place beef on rack in broiler pan. Broil with tops 4 to 6 inches from heat 6 minutes; turn. Broil 2 to 5 minutes longer for medium doneness. Serve with salsa.

1 serving: Calories 330 (Calories from Fat 125); Fat 14g (Saturated 6g); Cholesterol 110mg; Sodium 250mg; Carbohydrate 9g (Dietary Fiber 2g); Protein 44g

Betty's Tip

If you are a cilantro lover, increase the amount of cilantro in the salsa until you have just the amount you like.

MAKE IT A MEAL

Serve these steaks with hot flour tortillas.

Sirloin Steak with Caramelized Onions

4 SERVINGS PREP TIME: **8 MINUTES** START TO FINISH: **28 MINUTES**

1 tablespoon olive oil

2 large sweet onions, sliced (4 cups)

1 tablespoon Dijon mustard

1 teaspoon soy sauce

1 pound boneless beef sirloin steak, about 1 inch thick

⅛ teaspoon salt

¼ teaspoon pepper

Betty's Tip

Let food safety rule! Use a different plate and tongs to take raw food to the grill and to take cooked food from the grill.

1. Heat coals or gas grill.

2. Heat oil in 12-inch nonstick skillet over medium heat. Cook onions in oil 15 to 20 minutes, stirring occasionally, until onions are very soft and caramelized. Stir in mustard and soy sauce.

3. Meanwhile, sprinkle both sides of beef steak with salt and pepper. Place on grill. Cover grill and cook over medium heat 10 to 12 minutes for medium doneness, turning once.

4. Slice steak thinly across grain. Serve with onions.

1 serving: Calories 220 (Calories from Fat 70); Fat 7g (Saturated 1.5g); Cholesterol 65mg; Sodium 280mg; Carbohydrate 12g (Dietary Fiber 2g); Protein 27g

MAKE IT A MEAL

A salad of romaine lettuce, chopped tomatoes, and sliced cucumbers tossed with blue cheese dressing makes a fine companion to this special main dish.

Hungarian Swiss Steak

4 SERVINGS PREP TIME: **5 MINUTES** START TO FINISH: **35 MINUTES**

1 pound boneless beef sirloin steak, about ¾ inch thick

¼ teaspoon peppered seasoned salt

1 can (14½ ounces) stewed tomatoes, undrained

1 tablespoon paprika

2 tablespoons ketchup

¼ teaspoon caraway seed, if desired

½ cup reduced-fat sour cream

Chopped fresh chives, if desired

1. Remove fat from beef. Cut beef into 4 serving pieces. Sprinkle both sides of beef with seasoned salt.

2. Spray 12-inch nonstick skillet with cooking spray and heat over medium-high heat. Cook beef in skillet 4 to 8 minutes, turning once, until brown.

3. Stir in tomatoes, paprika, ketchup and caraway seed if desired; reduce heat. Cover and simmer 15 to 20 minutes or until beef is tender. Top each serving with sour cream and chives if desired.

1 serving: Calories 190 (Calories from Fat 45); Fat 5g (Saturated 2g); Cholesterol 65mg; Sodium 530mg; Carbohydrate 14g (Dietary Fiber 1g); Protein 23g

Betty's Tip

Paprika is made from ground sweet red pepper pods and can range from mild to hot. The color can vary as well, from bright orange to deep red. Many believe that Hungarian paprika is superior to all others.

MAKE IT A MEAL
Peas and Almonds

6 SERVINGS PREP TIME: **5 MINUTES** START TO FINISH: **13 MINUTES**

2 tablespoons butter or stick margarine

¼ cup slivered almonds

1 bag (1 pound) frozen green peas, thawed and drained

½ teaspoon salt

1. Melt butter in 10-inch skillet over medium heat. Cook almonds in butter 2 to 3 minutes, stirring occasionally, until light brown.

2. Stir in peas and salt. Cook 3 to 5 minutes, stirring frequently, until peas are tender.

1 serving: Calories 85 (Calories from Fat 45); Fat 5g (Saturated 2g); Cholesterol 5mg; Sodium 270mg; Carbohydrate 10g (Dietary Fiber 4g); Protein 4g

Beef Stroganoff Casserole

4 SERVINGS PREP TIME: **10 MINUTES** START TO FINISH: **1 HOUR**

1 pound boneless beef sirloin steak, about ½ inch thick

2 tablespoons margarine or butter

1 package (8 ounces) sliced mushrooms (3 cups)

1 medium onion, chopped (½ cup)

¾ cup beef broth

½ teaspoon Worcestershire sauce

¼ teaspoon salt

1 cup sour cream

1 cup Original Bisquick®

¼ cup milk

1 egg

Betty's Tip

Wild about mushrooms? Try sliced shiitake or portabella mushrooms for a rich and hearty flavor.

1. Heat oven to 400°. Grease 2½-quart casserole. Cut beef into 1 × ½-inch pieces. Melt margarine in 10-inch skillet over medium-high heat. Cook mushrooms and onion in margarine, stirring constantly, until onion is tender. Remove from skillet.

2. Cook beef in same skillet, stirring occasionally, until brown. Stir in broth, Worcestershire sauce and salt. Heat to boiling; reduce heat. Cover and simmer 15 minutes. Stir in mushroom mixture. Heat to boiling, stirring constantly, then remove from heat. Stir in sour cream. Spoon mixture into casserole.

3. Stir remaining ingredients in small bowl until blended. Spread evenly over beef mixture. Bake uncovered 20 to 25 minutes or until topping is golden brown. Let stand 5 minutes before serving.

1 serving: Calories 450 (Calories from Fat 235); Fat 26g (Saturated 11g); Cholesterol 145mg; Sodium 940mg; Carbohydrate 27g (Dietary Fiber 1g); Protein 28g

MAKE IT A MEAL

Stir frozen peas from a 10-ounce bag into the beef mixture in step 2.

Lemon Steak Diane

4 SERVINGS PREP TIME: **5 MINUTES** START TO FINISH: **20 MINUTES**

**1 pound boneless beef top sirloin steak,
about ¾ inch thick**

¼ teaspoon coarsely ground pepper

1 cup beef broth

1 tablespoon all-purpose flour

2 teaspoons Dijon mustard

2 teaspoons Worcestershire sauce

½ teaspoon grated lemon peel

2 tablespoons chopped fresh chives

1. Remove fat from beef. Cut beef into 4 pieces. Spray 12-inch nonstick skillet with cooking spray and heat over medium heat. Sprinkle both sides of beef with pepper. Cook beef in skillet 9 to 11 minutes for medium doneness, turning once. Remove beef from skillet and keep warm.

2. Mix remaining ingredients except chives until smooth and add to skillet. Heat to boiling. Boil 1 minute, stirring constantly. Stir in chives. Serve over beef.

1 serving: Calories 120 (Calories from Fat 25); Fat 3g (Saturated 1g); Cholesterol 55mg; Sodium 350mg; Carbohydrate 2g (Dietary Fiber 0g); Protein 21g

Betty's Tip

Worcestershire sauce gets its name from the place where it was first bottled, Worcester, England. What's in Worcestershire sauce? Garlic, soy sauce, tamarind, onions, molasses, lime, anchovies, vinegar and a variety of other seasonings. There is also a white Worcestershire sauce, which is light colored and less pungent.

Sweet-and-Sour Beef with Cabbage

4 SERVINGS PREP TIME: **10 MINUTES** START TO FINISH: **17 MINUTES**

2 tablespoons vegetable oil

1 pound cut-up beef for stir-fry

3 cups cut-up cabbage or coleslaw mix

½ cup sweet-and-sour sauce

Hot cooked couscous, rice or noodles, if desired

1. Heat wok or 12-inch skillet over high heat. Add 1 tablespoon of the oil and rotate wok to coat side.

2. Add beef and stir-fry 2 minutes or until brown. Remove beef from wok.

3. Add remaining 1 tablespoon oil to wok and rotate wok to coat side. Add cabbage and stir-fry about 3 minutes or until crisp-tender. Add beef and sweet-and-sour sauce. Cook and stir about 2 minutes or until hot. Serve with couscous if desired.

1 serving: Calories 225 (Calories from Fat 90); Fat 10g (Saturated 2g); Cholesterol 55mg; Sodium 150mg; Carbohydrate 13g (Dietary Fiber 1g); Protein 22g

Mexican Steak Stir-Fry

4 SERVINGS PREP TIME: **15 MINUTES** START TO FINISH: **25 MINUTES**

¾ pound boneless beef sirloin steak

1 medium onion, chopped (½ cup)

1 small green bell pepper, chopped (½ cup)

1 clove garlic, finely chopped

1 cup frozen whole kernel corn

½ cup salsa

1 medium zucchini, sliced (2 cups)

1 can (15 to 16 ounces) pinto beans, rinsed and drained

1 can (14½ ounces) whole tomatoes, undrained

1. Remove fat from beef. Cut beef into ¼ × ½-inch strips. (Beef is easier to cut if partially frozen, about 1½ hours.)

2. Spray 12-inch nonstick skillet or wok with cooking spray and heat over medium-high heat. Add beef, onion, bell pepper and garlic. Stir-fry 4 to 5 minutes or until beef is brown.

3. Stir in remaining ingredients, breaking up tomatoes. Cook about 5 minutes, stirring occasionally, until zucchini is tender and mixture is hot.

1 serving: Calories 240 (Calories from Fat 25); Fat 3g (Saturated 1g); Cholesterol 40mg; Sodium 390mg; Carbohydrate 38g (Dietary Fiber 10g); Protein 25g

Betty's Tip

Pinto beans are two-toned, kidney-shaped beans widely used in Central and South American cooking. They turn completely pink when cooked and are best known for their use in refried beans.

Stir-Fried Beef and Broccoli

4 SERVINGS PREP TIME: **14 MINUTES** START TO FINISH: **22 MINUTES**

½ cup cold water

2 tablespoons cornstarch

2 tablespoons soy sauce

1 pound boneless beef sirloin steak

2 tablespoons vegetable oil

¼ teaspoon ground ginger

¼ teaspoon garlic powder

1 bag (1 pound) frozen chopped broccoli, thawed and drained

1 cup orange juice

4 cups hot cooked rice

1. Mix water, cornstarch and soy sauce; set aside. Trim fat from beef. Cut beef with grain into 2-inch strips. Cut strips across grain into ⅛-inch slices.

2. Heat 12-inch skillet or wok over medium-high heat. Add oil and rotate skillet to coat bottom. Add beef, ginger and garlic powder. Stir-fry about 3 minutes or until beef is brown. Add broccoli and stir-fry 2 minutes.

3. Stir in orange juice and heat to boiling. Stir in cornstarch mixture. Cook and stir about 1 minute or until thickened. Serve beef mixture with rice.

1 serving: Calories 460 (Calories from Fat 100); Fat 11g (Saturated 2g); Cholesterol 55mg; Sodium 530mg; Carbohydrate 62g (Dietary Fiber 4g); Protein 28g

MAKE IT A MEAL

A fresh spinach salad with sliced red onion and mushrooms nicely complements this citrus-kissed stir-fry. For added zip, top the salad with crumbled Gorgonzola or blue cheese.

Korean Barbecued Beef

4 SERVINGS PREP TIME: **10 MINUTES** START TO FINISH: **43 MINUTES**

1 pound boneless beef top loin or sirloin steak

¼ cup soy sauce

3 tablespoons sugar

2 tablespoons sesame or vegetable oil

¼ teaspoon pepper

3 medium green onions, finely chopped (3 tablespoons)

2 cloves garlic, chopped

Hot cooked rice, if desired

1. Cut beef diagonally across grain into ⅛-inch slices. (Beef is easier to cut if partially frozen, about 1½ hours.)

2. Mix remaining ingredients except rice in medium glass or plastic bowl. Stir in beef until well coated. Cover and refrigerate 30 minutes.

3. Drain beef and discard marinade. Heat 10-inch skillet over medium heat. Cook beef in skillet 2 to 3 minutes, stirring frequently, until brown. Serve beef with rice if desired.

1 serving: Calories 260 (Calories from Fat 125); Fat 14g (Saturated 4g); Cholesterol 55mg; Sodium 1,080mg; Carbohydrate 12g (Dietary Fiber 0g); Protein 22g

MAKE IT A MEAL

Serve with steamed asparagus. Place steamer basket over ½ inch water (water should not touch bottom of basket). Place 1½ pounds trimmed and washed asparagus spears in basket. Cover tightly and heat to boiling; reduce heat. Steam 6 to 8 minutes or until crisp-tender.

Beef and Leeks in Spicy Chili Sauce

4 SERVINGS PREP TIME: **10 MINUTES** START TO FINISH: **17 MINUTES**

1 tablespoon chili oil or vegetable oil

1 pound boneless beef sirloin steak, cut into ¼-inch strips

2 leeks, thinly sliced (2 cups)

1 bag (1 pound) frozen broccoli, carrots, water chestnuts and red peppers

1 tablespoon chili puree with garlic

Hot cooked rice or noodles, if desired

1. Heat wok or 12-inch skillet over high heat. Add oil and rotate wok to coat side.

2. Add beef and leeks and stir-fry 2 minutes. Add vegetables and stir-fry about 4 minutes or until beef is brown and vegetables are crisp-tender.

3. Stir in chili puree. Cook and stir about 30 seconds or until hot. Serve with rice if desired.

1 serving: Calories 185 (Calories from Fat 65); Fat 7g (Saturated 2g); Cholesterol 55mg; Sodium 125mg; Carbohydrate 11g (Dietary Fiber 4g); Protein 23g

Sirloin Three-Bean Chili

8 SERVINGS PREP TIME: **35 MINUTES** START TO FINISH: **55 MINUTES**

1 tablespoon canola oil

2 pounds boneless beef sirloin steak, cut into 1-inch cubes

1 large onion, coarsely chopped (1 cup)

1 medium green bell pepper, coarsely chopped (1 cup)

2 cans (28 ounces each) diced tomatoes, undrained

1 can (15 to 16 ounces) pinto beans, rinsed and drained

1 can (15 to 16 ounces) kidney beans, rinsed and drained

1 can (15 ounces) black beans, rinsed and drained

1 cup beef broth

1½ tablespoons ground cumin

1 tablespoon chili powder

1. Heat oil in 4-quart Dutch oven over medium-high heat. Cook 1 pound of beef at a time in oil, stirring occasionally, until brown. Remove from Dutch oven.

2. Add onion and bell pepper to Dutch oven. Cook 2 to 3 minutes, stirring occasionally, until crisp-tender. Stir in remaining ingredients except beef.

3. Cover and cook over medium heat 10 minutes. Stir in beef. Cook uncovered 3 to 8 minutes or until beef is tender.

1 serving: Calories 410 (Calories from Fat 60); Fat 7g (Saturated 1.5g); Cholesterol 65mg; Sodium 430mg; Carbohydrate 46g (Dietary Fiber 13g); Protein 41g

MAKE IT A MEAL

Serve with hot corn bread from the oven.

Beef, Lettuce and Tomato Wraps

4 SERVINGS PREP TIME: **30 MINUTES** START TO FINISH: **50 MINUTES**

1 tablespoon plus 1½ teaspoons chili powder

2 teaspoons dried oregano leaves

1 teaspoon ground cumin

1 teaspoon salt

1 pound beef top sirloin steak, about ¾ inch thick

4 whole wheat tortillas (6 to 8 inches in diameter)

¾ cup reduced-fat sour cream

1 tablespoon prepared horseradish

4 cups shredded lettuce

1 large tomato, chopped (1 cup)

1. Mix chili powder, oregano, cumin and salt in small bowl. Rub mixture on both sides of beef. Let stand 10 minutes at room temperature.

2. Set oven control to broil. Place beef on rack in broiler pan. Broil with top 3 to 4 inches from heat for about 10 minutes for medium doneness, turning once, or until desired doneness. Cut into ⅛-inch slices.

3. Warm tortillas as directed on package. Mix sour cream and horseradish in small bowl. Spread 3 tablespoons horseradish mixture over each tortilla. Top each with 1 cup of the lettuce and ¼ cup of the tomato. Top with beef. Wrap tortillas around filling.

1 serving: Calories 280 (Calories from Fat 90); Fat 10g (Saturated 5g); Cholesterol 80mg; Sodium 790mg; Carbohydrate 17g (Dietary Fiber 4g); Protein 30g

Betty's Tip

Your supermarket likely offers many whole grain options. Look for whole wheat tortillas, which are a great alternative to the white ones. Besides being a whole grain, they have more flavor and texture.

Roast Beef and Swiss Sandwich Bake

6 SERVINGS PREP TIME: **10 MINUTES** START TO FINISH: **1 HOUR 5 MINUTES**

2 cups Original Bisquick®

1 cup milk

2 tablespoons yellow mustard

1 egg

1 package (6 ounces) thinly sliced cooked roast beef, chopped

1 cup shredded Swiss cheese (4 ounces)

Freshly ground pepper, if desired

Betty's Tip

Vary this dish by using thinly sliced cooked turkey or chicken instead of roast beef, and shredded Cheddar cheese instead of Swiss.

1. Heat oven to 350°. Grease square baking dish, 8 × 8 × 2 inches.

2. Stir Bisquick, milk, mustard and egg until blended. Pour half of the batter into baking dish. Top with half of the roast beef and ½ cup of the cheese. Top with remaining roast beef. Pour remaining batter over roast beef.

3. Bake uncovered 45 to 50 minutes or until golden brown and center is set. Sprinkle with remaining ½ cup cheese and the pepper if desired. Let stand 5 minutes before serving.

1 serving: Calories 330 (Calories from Fat 155); Fat 17g (Saturated 7g); Cholesterol 75mg; Sodium 730mg; Carbohydrate 27g (Dietary Fiber 1g); Protein 18g

MAKE IT A MEAL

Prepare your favorite coleslaw or purchase some from the delicatessen.

Skillet Hash

4 SERVINGS PREP TIME: **10 MINUTES** START TO FINISH: **25 MINUTES**

2 cups chopped cooked lean beef or corned beef

2 cups frozen country-style hash brown potatoes

1 medium onion, chopped (½ cup)

1 tablespoon chopped fresh parsley

½ teaspoon salt

⅛ teaspoon pepper

2 to 3 tablespoons vegetable oil

1. Mix beef, potatoes, onion, parsley, salt and pepper.

2. Heat oil in 10-inch skillet over medium heat. Spread beef mixture evenly in skillet. Cook 10 to 15 minutes, turning frequently, until brown.

1 serving: Calories 307 (Calories from Fat 125); Fat 14g (Saturated 4g); Cholesterol 6mg; Sodium 362mg; Carbohydrate 21g (Dietary Fiber 2g); Protein 24g

MAKE IT A MEAL

Serve poached or scrambled eggs with the hash for a quick and comforting meal.

Italian Beef and Vegetable Soup

5 SERVINGS PREP TIME: **20 MINUTES** START TO FINISH: **48 MINUTES**

2 teaspoons all-purpose flour

¼ teaspoon salt

¼ teaspoon pepper

½ pound boneless beef round steak, cut into ½-inch cubes

1 tablespoon olive oil

1 can (15 ounces) cannellini beans, rinsed and drained

1 can (14½ ounces) diced tomatoes with basil, garlic and oregano, undrained

2 cups frozen Italian-blend vegetables

3 cups water

Grated Parmesan cheese, if desired

1. Place flour, salt and pepper in 1-quart resealable plastic food-storage bag. Seal bag and shake until blended. Add beef. Seal bag and shake until beef is evenly coated with flour mixture.

2. Heat oil in 3-quart heavy saucepan or Dutch oven over medium-high heat. Cook beef in oil 4 to 5 minutes, stirring occasionally, until brown on all sides.

3. Stir in remaining ingredients except cheese. Heat to boiling; reduce heat. Simmer uncovered 15 to 20 minutes or until vegetables are tender. Serve with cheese if desired.

1 serving: Calories 220 (Calories from Fat 40); Fat 4.5g (Saturated 1g); Cholesterol 25mg; Sodium 250mg; Carbohydrate 25g (Dietary Fiber 7g); Protein 19g

*Betty's Tip*_____

Eating soup is a great way to work in vegetables without even noticing it.

MAKE IT A MEAL

Use refrigerated or frozen dough to make quick breadsticks. Serve hot from the oven with the soup.

Beef and Millet Stew in Bread Bowls

6 SERVINGS PREP TIME: **20 MINUTES** START TO FINISH: **1 HOUR 35 MINUTES**

BREAD BOWLS

1 loaf (about 1 pound) frozen 100% whole wheat bread dough, thawed

1 tablespoon olive oil

1 teaspoon dried basil leaves

STEW

2 teaspoons olive oil

1 pound lean beef stew meat, cut into small pieces

1 medium onion, chopped (½ cup)

2 cloves garlic, finely chopped

2 teaspoons dried herbes de Provence

½ teaspoon salt

¼ teaspoon pepper

1 can (14 ounces) reduced-sodium beef broth

1 can (28 ounces) diced tomatoes, undrained

½ cup water

½ cup uncooked millet

1 cup baby carrots, cut in half lengthwise

1 cup frozen cut green beans

Betty's Tip

You can substitute 1 teaspoon dried basil leaves plus 1 teaspoon dried rosemary leaves for the herbes de Provence.

1. Lightly grease outsides of 6 (10-ounce) custard cups with shortening. (Do not use cooking spray.) Place cups upside down on large cookie sheet.

2. Divide dough into 6 equal pieces. Shape each piece into ball. Roll or pat each ball into 6-inch round. Place dough round over bottom of each custard cup, stretching to fit. Brush dough with 1 tablespoon oil and sprinkle with basil. Cover and let rise in warm place 20 minutes.

3. Heat oven to 350°. Bake bread bowls 16 to 20 minutes or until golden brown. Cool 5 minutes, then remove from cups to cooling rack. Cool completely, about 30 minutes. (Interiors of bread bowls may be slightly moist.)

4. Meanwhile, heat 2 teaspoons oil in 3-quart saucepan over medium-high heat. Add beef, onion, garlic, herbes de Provence, salt and pepper. Cook 5 to 6 minutes, stirring occasionally, until beef is lightly browned.

5. Stir in broth, tomatoes and water. Heat to boiling. Reduce heat to low. Cover and simmer 45 minutes. Stir in millet, carrots and green beans. Cook uncovered about 25 minutes or until beef is tender. Serve stew in bread bowls.

1 serving: Calories 490 (Calories from Fat 160); Fat 17g (Saturated 5g); Cholesterol 45mg; Sodium 870mg; Carbohydrate 58g (Dietary Fiber 9g); Protein 26g

Southwestern Beef on Biscuits

10 SERVINGS PREP TIME: **15 MINUTES** START TO FINISH: **30 MINUTES**

Biscuits (right)

1 tub (32 ounces) fully cooked barbeque sauce with sliced beef

1 can (11 ounces) whole kernel corn with red and green peppers, drained

1 can (2¼ ounces) sliced ripe olives, drained

½ cup shredded Cheddar or Colby cheese (2 ounces)

⅓ cup sour cream

1. Make Biscuits.

2. While biscuits are baking, heat beef mixture in 4-quart saucepan over medium heat 10 to 12 minutes, stirring occasionally, until hot. Stir in corn and olives and heat until hot.

3. Split warm biscuits. Place 1 half biscuit, cut side up, on each serving plate. Spoon beef mixture over biscuit halves. Sprinkle with cheese. Top with sour cream.

BISCUITS

3¼ cups Original Bisquick®

1 cup milk

1. Heat oven to 450°.

2. Stir Bisquick and milk until soft dough forms. Place on surface dusted with Bisquick. Knead 10 times. Roll dough ½ inch thick. Cut with 4-inch cutter to make 5 biscuits.

3. Place on ungreased cookie sheet. Bake 11 to 14 minutes or until golden brown.

1 serving: Calories 430 (Calories from Fat 200); Fat 22g (Saturated 6g); Cholesterol 40mg; Sodium 1,310mg; Carbohydrate 34g (Dietary Fiber 2g); Protein 26g

MAKE IT A MEAL

Turn this easy dish into a weeknight fiesta with additional toppings such as shredded lettuce, chopped tomatoes, sliced green onions and guacamole.

Beef Cube Steaks with Mushroom-Cream Sauce

4 SERVINGS PREP TIME: **10 MINUTES** START TO FINISH: **25 MINUTES**

4 beef cube steaks (4 ounces each)

½ teaspoon salt

½ teaspoon pepper

3 tablespoons vegetable oil

1 package (8 ounces) sliced mushrooms (3 cups)

1 cup sour cream with chives

1. Sprinkle both sides of beef steaks with salt and pepper. Heat 2 tablespoons of the oil in 10-inch nonstick skillet over medium-high heat. Cook beef in oil 5 to 6 minutes for medium doneness, turning once. Remove beef from skillet and keep warm.

2. Heat remaining 1 tablespoon oil and drippings in skillet over medium-high heat. Cook mushrooms in oil, stirring occasionally, until liquid evaporates. Reduce heat to medium.

3. Stir in sour cream and cook until hot. Do not boil. Serve over beef.

1 serving: Calories 413 (Calories from Fat 285); Fat 32g (Saturated 13g); Cholesterol 72mg; Sodium 385mg; Carbohydrate 5g (Dietary Fiber 1g); Protein 28g

MAKE IT A MEAL

Serve over spinach fettuccine with a spinach salad tossed with crumbled bacon, mandarin orange segments and poppy seed dressing.

Quick Brandied Steak with Pepper

4 SERVINGS PREP TIME: **10 MINUTES** START TO FINISH: **25 MINUTES**

1 teaspoon cracked black pepper

¾ teaspoon chopped fresh or ¼ teaspoon dried basil leaves

¾ teaspoon chopped fresh or ¼ teaspoon dried rosemary leaves

⅛ teaspoon onion powder

4 beef cube steaks (5 ounces each)

1 tablespoon margarine or butter

2 tablespoons brandy or beef broth

¼ cup beef broth

1. Mix pepper, basil, rosemary and onion powder. Rub pepper mixture into both sides of each steak.

2. Melt margarine in 12-inch skillet over medium heat. Cook beef in margarine 7 to 8 minutes, turning occasionally, until medium-rare to medium. Remove beef from skillet and keep warm.

3. Add brandy and broth to skillet. Heat to boiling, stirring to loosen brown bits from bottom of skillet. Reduce heat to low and simmer uncovered 3 to 4 minutes or until slightly thickened. Pour brandy mixture over beef.

1 serving: Calories 279 (Calories from Fat 132); Fat 15g (Saturated 5g); Cholesterol 58mg; Sodium 166mg; Carbohydrate 1g (Dietary Fiber 0g); Protein 30g

MAKE IT A MEAL

Spoon canned lemon pie filling into miniature graham cracker crusts (in individual foil tins). Add a generous dollop of real whipped cream or nondairy whipped topping.

Speedy Beef Stew

6 SERVINGS PREP TIME: **10 MINUTES** START TO FINISH: **40 MINUTES**

1 pound beef cube steaks

2 teaspoons vegetable oil

3 cups beef broth

1 cup baby carrots

1 cup frozen small whole onions, thawed

2 teaspoons caraway seed

⅛ teaspoon pepper

1 pound small red potatoes, cut into fourths

1 jar (**12 ounces**) baby corn, drained

3 tablespoons cornstarch

1. Cut beef steaks into 1-inch squares. Heat oil in 3-quart saucepan or Dutch oven over medium-high heat. Cook beef in oil about 5 minutes, stirring frequently, until brown.

2. Stir in 2½ cups of the broth, the carrots, onions, caraway seed, pepper and potatoes. Heat to boiling; reduce heat. Cover and simmer about 20 minutes or until beef and vegetables are tender. Stir in corn.

3. Mix cornstarch and remaining ½ cup broth. Stir into stew. Cook about 3 minutes, stirring constantly, until thickened.

1 serving (3 squares each): Calories 286 (Calories from Fat 82); Fat 9g (Saturated 3g); Cholesterol 31mg; Sodium 515mg; Carbohydrate 31g (Dietary Fiber 4g); Protein 21g

Skillet Hot Tamale Pie

6 SERVINGS PREP TIME: **10 MINUTES** START TO FINISH: **27 MINUTES**

½ cup yellow cornmeal

½ cup cold water

1⅓ cups water

1 pound lean ground beef

1 large onion, chopped (1 cup)

1 medium green or red bell pepper, chopped (1 cup)

1 can (15 to 16 ounces) reduced-sodium kidney beans, rinsed and drained

1 can (10 ounces) enchilada sauce

½ cup shredded reduced-fat Cheddar cheese (2 ounces)

SPEED SUPPER
With this cornmeal-topped pie, you can enjoy tamale-like flavor without the time-consuming work of filling and steaming authentic tamales.

1. Mix cornmeal and ½ cup cold water; set aside. Heat 1⅓ cups water to boiling in 2-quart saucepan. Gradually add cornmeal mixture to boiling water, stirring constantly to make sure it does not lump. Heat to boiling, stirring constantly, then reduce heat to low. Simmer uncovered about 10 minutes, stirring occasionally, until very thick.

2. While cornmeal mixture is cooking, cook beef, onion and bell pepper in 12-inch nonstick skillet over medium heat about 6 minutes, stirring occasionally, until beef is brown; drain. Stir in kidney beans and enchilada sauce.

3. Spoon hot cornmeal mixture on beef mixture in a ring around edge of skillet. Cover and simmer about 5 minutes longer or until heated through. Sprinkle with cheese.

1 serving: Calories 290 (Calories from Fat 90); Fat 10g (Saturated 4g); Cholesterol 45mg; Sodium 390mg; Carbohydrate 31g (Dietary Fiber 7g); Protein 26g

Betty's Tip
If you like, substitute ground turkey breast or lean ground pork for the ground beef.

Easy Picadillo

4 SERVINGS PREP TIME: **5 MINUTES** START TO FINISH: **22 MINUTES**

1 pound lean ground beef

1 small green bell pepper, chopped (½ cup)

1 can (14½ ounces) salsa-style chunky tomatoes, undrained

1 cup canned black beans, rinsed and drained

½ cup golden raisins

Betty's Tip

Picadillo is a favorite dish of Spanish-speaking countries. Ingredients vary, but usually include ground meat, tomatoes and onions. This tasty version contains black beans, which are traditional with Cuban picadillo.

1. Cook beef and bell pepper in 12-inch nonstick skillet over medium heat 8 to 10 minutes, stirring occasionally, until beef is brown; drain.

2. Stir in remaining ingredients and reduce heat to low. Cover and simmer 5 to 7 minutes, stirring occasionally, until hot.

1 serving: Calories 365 (Calories from Fat 155); Fat 17g (Saturated 7g); Cholesterol 65mg; Sodium 330mg; Carbohydrate 32g (Dietary Fiber 5g); Protein 26g

MAKE IT A MEAL

Serve this easy supper over cooked rice. End the meal with chunks of fresh melon.

Salsa Salisbury Steak

4 SERVINGS PREP TIME: 10 MINUTES START TO FINISH: 25 MINUTES

1 pound lean ground beef

1 medium onion, finely chopped (½ cup)

½ teaspoon chili powder

¼ teaspoon garlic salt

1 can (14½ ounces) salsa-style chunky tomatoes, undrained

1. Mix beef, onion, chili powder and garlic salt. Shape mixture into 4 oblong patties.

2. Spray 12-inch nonstick skillet with cooking spray and heat over medium-high heat. Cook patties in skillet 3 to 5 minutes, turning once, until brown; drain.

3. Stir in tomatoes and reduce heat to low. Cover and simmer about 10 minutes, stirring tomatoes occasionally and turning patties once, until beef is no longer pink in center and juice of beef is clear.

1 serving: Calories 255 (Calories from Fat 145); Fat 16g (Saturated 7g); Cholesterol 65mg; Sodium 280mg; Carbohydrate 7g (Dietary Fiber 1g); Protein 22g

MAKE IT A MEAL

Serve on a bed of hot mashed potatoes.

Beef and Kasha Mexicana

6 SERVINGS PREP TIME: **10 MINUTES** START TO FINISH: **29 MINUTES**

1 pound lean ground beef

1 medium onion, chopped (½ cup)

1 cup uncooked kasha (roasted buckwheat groats)

1 can (14½ ounces) diced tomatoes, undrained

1 can (4½ ounces) chopped green chilies, undrained

1 package (1.25 ounces) 40%-less-sodium taco seasoning mix

2 cups frozen whole kernel corn, thawed

1½ cups water

1 cup shredded reduced-fat Cheddar cheese (4 ounces)

2 tablespoons chopped fresh cilantro, if desired

2 tablespoons sliced ripe olives, if desired

1. Cook beef and onion in 12-inch skillet over medium-high heat 5 to 7 minutes, stirring occasionally, until beef is brown; drain. Stir in kasha until kernels are moistened by beef mixture.

2. Stir in tomatoes, chilies, taco seasoning mix, corn and water. Heat to boiling. Cover and reduce heat to low. Simmer 5 to 7 minutes, stirring occasionally, until kasha is tender.

3. Sprinkle cheese over kasha mixture. Cover and cook 2 to 3 minutes or until cheese is melted. Sprinkle with cilantro and olives if desired.

1 serving: Calories 300 (Calories from Fat 80); Fat 9g (Saturated 3.5g); Cholesterol 50mg; Sodium 990mg; Carbohydrate 33g (Dietary Fiber 5g); Protein 23g

Betty's Tip

You can also use this mixture as a filling for tortillas.

Bacon Cheeseburgers

6 SERVINGS PREP TIME: **10 MINUTES** START TO FINISH: **20 MINUTES**

¼ cup fat-free cholesterol-free egg product or 2 egg whites

1 tablespoon ketchup

1 tablespoon Dijon mustard

¼ cup dry bread crumbs

2 tablespoons bacon-flavor bits or chips

¼ teaspoon ground red pepper (cayenne)

1 pound lean ground beef

3 slices reduced-fat process Cheddar or American cheese product, cut diagonally in half

Lettuce leaves, if desired

Tomato slices, if desired

Hamburger buns, split and toasted, if desired

1. Set oven control to broil. Spray broiler pan rack with cooking spray.

2. Mix egg product, ketchup and mustard in large bowl. Stir in bread crumbs, bacon bits and red pepper. Stir in beef. Shape mixture into 6 patties, each about ½ inch thick.

3. Place patties on rack in broiler pan. Broil with tops about 5 inches from heat about 5 minutes on each side for medium, turning once, until no longer pink in center and juice is clear. Immediately top with cheese. Serve with lettuce and tomato on buns if desired.

1 serving: Calories 185 (Calories from Fat 90); Fat 10g (Saturated 4g); Cholesterol 45mg; Sodium 260mg; Carbohydrate 5g (Dietary Fiber 1g); Protein 20g

Betty's Tip

Add a little fire to the burger by using hot-style ketchup.

Sauerbraten Burgers

4 SERVINGS PREP TIME: **10 MINUTES** START TO FINISH: **25 MINUTES**

1 pound ground beef

6 gingersnaps, finely crushed

1 small onion, finely chopped (¼ cup)

¼ teaspoon ground ginger

1 jar (**12 ounces**) brown gravy

¼ cup red wine vinegar

2 tablespoons packed brown sugar

¼ cup raisins

SPEED SUPPER
Sauerbraten is a traditional German specialty that takes two to three days to make. Our super-quick version uses ground beef and purchased gravy, and keeps all the great taste.

1. Mix beef, 2 tablespoons of the cookie crumbs, the onion and ginger. Shape mixture into 4 patties, each about ½-inch thick.

2. Spray 12-inch nonstick skillet with cooking spray and heat over medium-high heat. Cook patties in skillet 5 minutes, turning once, until brown; drain.

3. Meanwhile, mix gravy, vinegar and brown sugar in small bowl. Stir in remaining cookie crumbs and the raisins. Pour over patties in skillet. Reduce heat to medium-low. Cook uncovered about 10 minutes, stirring occasionally, until gravy is desired consistency, beef is no longer pink in center and juice of beef is clear.

1 serving: Calories 385 (Calories from Fat 170); Fat 19g (Saturated 8g); Cholesterol 65mg; Sodium 590mg; Carbohydrate 29g (Dietary Fiber 1g); Protein 25g

MAKE IT A MEAL
Serve with steamed green beans.

Mini Meat Loaves

4 SERVINGS PREP TIME: **10 MINUTES** START TO FINISH: **35 MINUTES**

1 pound lean ground beef

½ cup dry bread crumbs

¼ cup milk

½ teaspoon salt

½ teaspoon Worcestershire sauce, if desired

¼ teaspoon pepper

1 small onion, finely chopped

1 egg

1. Heat oven to 400°.

2. Mix all ingredients. Pat mixture in rectangle, 9 × 3 inches, in ungreased rectangular baking dish. Cut into 1½-inch squares and separate squares slightly.

3. Bake uncovered about 25 minutes or until no longer pink in center and juice is clear (meat thermometer should reach at least 160°).

1 serving (3 squares each): Calories 287 (Calories from Fat 124); Fat 14g (Saturated 5g); Cholesterol 128mg; Sodium 489mg; Carbohydrate 12g (Dietary Fiber 1g); Protein 27g

Betty's Tip

This recipe can also be used for meatballs. Shape and cut meat mixture as directed, except shape into balls. Cook meatballs in 10-inch skillet over medium heat about 20 minutes, turning occasionally, until no longer pink in center and juice is clear.

MAKE IT A MEAL

For a sweet and sassy fruit salad, stir 1 tablespoon canned green chilies or fresh jalapeño pepper into a can of undrained fruit cocktail or tropical fruit blend.

Mini Greek Meat Loaves with Tzatziki Sauce

4 SERVINGS PREP TIME: **20 MINUTES** START TO FINISH: **1 HOUR**

MEAT LOAVES

1 pound lean ground beef

½ box (9-ounce size) frozen spinach, cooked and well drained (about ½ cup)

1 small onion, finely chopped (¼ cup)

⅓ cup quick-cooking or old-fashioned oats

2 ounces crumbled feta cheese (½ cup)

1 egg plus 1 egg white

1 teaspoon dried oregano leaves, crushed

½ teaspoon garlic salt

¼ teaspoon pepper

SAUCE

¾ cup plain low-fat yogurt

½ medium cucumber, peeled, seeded and finely chopped (½ cup)

1 tablespoon olive oil

¼ teaspoon salt

1 clove garlic, finely chopped

1. Heat oven to 350°. Spray 8 regular-size muffin cups with cooking spray.

2. Mix all meat loaves ingredients in medium bowl. Scoop generous ⅓ cup meat mixture into each muffin cup, pressing down slightly.

3. Bake 30 to 35 minutes or until no longer pink in centers of loaves (meat thermometer should reach at least 160°). Let stand in pan 5 minutes.

4. Meanwhile, mix all sauce ingredients in small bowl. Refrigerate until serving. Serve sauce with meat loaves.

1 serving: Calories 330 (Calories from Fat 160); Fat 18g (Saturated 7g); Cholesterol 140mg; Sodium 560mg; Carbohydrate 12g (Dietary Fiber 2g); Protein 31g

Betty's Tip

Tzatziki is a typical Greek sauce and is a nice complement to the meat loaves and cooked green leafy vegetables.

Italian Roasted Pork Tenderloin

6 SERVINGS PREP TIME: **10 MINUTES** START TO FINISH: **45 MINUTES**

2 pork tenderloins, about ¾ pound each

1 teaspoon olive or vegetable oil

½ teaspoon salt

½ teaspoon fennel seed, crushed

¼ teaspoon pepper

1 clove garlic, finely chopped

1. Heat oven to 375°. Spray roasting pan rack with cooking spray. Remove fat from pork. Mash remaining ingredients into a paste. Rub paste on pork.

2. Place pork on rack in shallow roasting pan. Insert meat thermometer so tip is in center of thickest part of pork. Roast uncovered about 35 minutes or until thermometer reads 160°.

1 serving: Calories 140 (Calories from Fat 45); Fat 5g (Saturated 2g); Cholesterol 65mg; Sodium 240mg; Carbohydrate 0g (Dietary Fiber 0g); Protein 24g

Pork Tenderloin with Apples and Sweet Potatoes

6 SERVINGS PREP TIME: 15 MINUTES START TO FINISH: 1 HOUR 15 MINUTES

¼ cup packed brown sugar

¼ cup butter or margarine, melted

1 tablespoon cider vinegar

1 teaspoon salt

½ teaspoon garlic powder

½ teaspoon pepper

2 medium red cooking apples, sliced (about 2 cups)

2 medium dark-orange sweet potatoes, peeled and thinly sliced (about 2½ cups)

1 medium onion, chopped (½ cup)

2 pork tenderloins (1 pound each)

Betty's Tip

Be sure to use pork tenderloins—not pork loins—in this recipe. Pork loins are much larger and less tender, and would take longer to cook.

1. Heat oven to 425°. Mix brown sugar, butter, vinegar, salt, garlic powder and pepper in medium bowl. Reserve 2 tablespoons of the butter mixture. Add apples, sweet potatoes and onion to remaining butter mixture and toss to coat. Spread apple mixture in roasting pan or rectangular baking dish, 13 × 9 × 2 inches. Cover tightly with aluminum foil and bake 20 minutes.

2. Meanwhile, brush pork with reserved butter mixture. Heat 10-inch nonstick skillet over medium-high heat until hot. Cook pork in skillet about 3 minutes, turning to brown all sides evenly.

3. Place pork on apple mixture. Bake uncovered 30 to 40 minutes or until pork is slightly pink in center and meat thermometer inserted in center of thickest part reads 160°.

1 serving: Calories 360 (Calories from Fat 120); Fat 14g (Saturated 7g); Cholesterol 115mg; Sodium 540mg; Carbohydrate 25g (Dietary Fiber 3g); Protein 35g

Sesame Pork with Garlic Cream Sauce

6 SERVINGS PREP TIME: **5 MINUTES** START TO FINISH: **20 MINUTES**

1½ pounds pork tenderloin

1 tablespoon vegetable oil

1 tablespoon sesame seed

1 tablespoon margarine, butter or spread

2 cloves garlic, finely chopped

1 package (3 ounces) cream cheese, cut into cubes

⅓ cup milk

1 tablespoon chopped fresh or 1 teaspoon freeze-dried chives

1. Cut pork into ½-inch slices.

2. Set oven control to broil. Brush oil over pork. Place pork on rack in broiler pan. Sprinkle with half of the sesame seed. Broil pork with tops 4 to 6 inches from heat 6 minutes; turn. Sprinkle with remaining sesame seed. Broil about 5 minutes longer or until no longer pink.

3. Meanwhile, melt margarine in 10-inch skillet over medium heat. Cook garlic in margarine about 2 minutes, stirring occasionally, until softened. Reduce heat to low.

4. Stir cream cheese and milk into garlic mixture. Cook about 1 minute, stirring constantly, until smooth and hot. Stir in chives. Serve with pork.

1 serving: Calories 240 (Calories from Fat 125); Fat 14g (Saturated 6g); Cholesterol 85mg; Sodium 120mg; Carbohydrate 2g (Dietary Fiber 0g); Protein 26g

MAKE IT A MEAL

Sautéed baby spinach is a fresh, fast accompaniment.

Caramelized Pork Slices

4 SERVINGS PREP TIME: **10 MINUTES** START TO FINISH: **20 MINUTES**

1 pound pork tenderloin

2 cloves garlic, finely chopped

2 tablespoons packed brown sugar

1 tablespoon orange juice

1 tablespoon molasses

½ teaspoon salt

¼ teaspoon pepper

1. Remove fat from pork. Cut pork into ½-inch slices.

2. Spray 10-inch nonstick skillet with cooking spray and heat over medium-high heat. Cook pork and garlic in skillet 6 to 8 minutes, turning occasionally, until pork is slightly pink in center. Drain if necessary.

3. Stir in remaining ingredients. Cook until mixture thickens and coats pork.

1 serving: Calories 175 (Calories from Fat 35); Fat 4g (Saturated 2g); Cholesterol 65mg; Sodium 350mg; Carbohydrate 11g (Dietary Fiber 0g); Protein 24g

MAKE IT A MEAL

Serve this slightly sweet roast pork with corn and baked or mashed sweet potatoes.

Pork with Sweet Mustard Gravy

4 SERVINGS PREP TIME: **5 MINUTES** START TO FINISH: **15 MINUTES**

1 pound pork tenderloin, cut into ¼-inch slices

¼ teaspoon peppered seasoned salt

1 jar (12 ounces) pork gravy

2 tablespoons red currant jelly

1 teaspoon ground mustard

1 medium green onion, sliced (1 tablespoon)

1. Spray 12-inch nonstick skillet with cooking spray and heat over medium heat. Sprinkle both sides of pork slices with seasoned salt. Cook pork in skillet about 5 minutes, turning once, until brown.

2. Stir in gravy, jelly, mustard and onion. Heat to boiling, then reduce heat to medium. Cook 3 to 4 minutes, stirring occasionally, until sauce is desired consistency and pork is no longer pink.

1 serving: Calories 205 (Calories from Fat 55); Fat 6g (Saturated 3g); Cholesterol 70mg; Sodium 610mg; Carbohydrate 11g (Dietary Fiber 0g); Protein 27g

MAKE IT A MEAL

Serve this 15-minute meal with rice and fresh broccoli spears.

Nut-Crusted Pork Medallions

4 SERVINGS PREP TIME: **10 MINUTES** START TO FINISH: **18 MINUTES**

1 egg

¼ cup honey

¾ to 1 pound pork tenderloin, cut into ½-inch slices

1 cup chopped pecans

½ cup yellow cornmeal

1 teaspoon salt

½ teaspoon pepper

2 tablespoons vegetable oil

1. Mix egg and honey in small bowl. Add pork and toss to coat.

2. Place pecans, cornmeal, salt and pepper in food processor. Cover and process until finely chopped. Place pecan mixture in resealable plastic food-storage bag. Add pork, seal bag and shake to coat.

3. Heat oil in 10-inch nonstick skillet over medium-high heat. Cook pork in oil 6 to 8 minutes, turning once, until golden brown on outside and no longer pink in center.

1 serving: Calories 496 (Calories from Fat 286); Fat 32g (Saturated 4g); Cholesterol 105mg; Sodium 648mg; Carbohydrate 33g (Dietary Fiber 4g); Protein 23g

Betty's Tip

If you like sweet-and-hot and sweet-and-salty flavors, add a dash of hot pepper sauce to the honey and egg mixture in step 1.

MAKE IT A MEAL

Add corn on the cob and baking powder biscuits to complete the meal.

Rosemary Pork Roast with Carrots

8 SERVINGS PREP TIME: **15 MINUTES** START TO FINISH: **1 HOUR 45 MINUTES**

1 boneless pork center loin roast
(about 2½ pounds)

3 teaspoons canola oil

2 teaspoons dried rosemary leaves, crumbled

1 teaspoon salt

¼ teaspoon pepper

2 pounds baby carrots

1 large sweet onion, cut into 16 wedges

½ teaspoon garlic powder

1. Heat oven to 400°. Spray 15 × 10 × 1-inch pan with cooking spray. Remove fat from pork. Rub pork with 1 teaspoon of the oil. Sprinkle with 1 teaspoon of the rosemary, ½ teaspoon of the salt and the pepper. Place in center of pan. Insert meat thermometer so tip is in center of thickest part of pork.

2. Mix carrots, onion, garlic powder, and remaining 2 teaspoons oil, 1 teaspoon rosemary and ½ teaspoon salt in large bowl. Arrange carrot mixture around pork.

3. Roast uncovered 1 hour to 1 hour 30 minutes or until thermometer reads 160° and vegetables are tender. Cover with tent of aluminum foil and let stand about 10 minutes before carving.

1 serving: Calories 300 (Calories from Fat 120); Fat 13g (Saturated 4g); Cholesterol 90mg; Sodium 430mg; Carbohydrate 13g (Dietary Fiber 4g); Protein 33g

Apple-Rosemary Pork and Rice

4 SERVINGS PREP TIME: **10 MINUTES** START TO FINISH: **25 MINUTES**

1½ cups apple juice

1½ cups uncooked instant rice

2 tablespoons chopped fresh or 2 teaspoons crumbled dried rosemary leaves

2 teaspoons vegetable oil

¾ pound pork tenderloin, cut into ½-inch slices

1 medium onion, chopped (½ cup)

1 clove garlic, finely chopped

¼ cup apple jelly

1 large unpeeled red cooking apple, sliced

Rosemary sprigs, if desired

Betty's Tip

Experience the amazingly good flavor of toasted pecans or walnuts. Sprinkle them on top of the pork and rice just before serving.

1. Heat apple juice to boiling in 2-quart saucepan. Stir in rice and 1 tablespoon of the rosemary; remove from heat. Cover and let stand until ready to serve. Just before serving, fluff with fork.

2. Heat oil in 10-inch nonstick skillet over medium-high heat. Cook pork, onion, garlic and remaining 1 tablespoon rosemary in oil 6 to 8 minutes, stirring occasionally, until pork is slightly pink in center.

3. Stir in apply jelly and apple and cook until hot. Serve over rice. Garnish with rosemary sprigs if desired.

1 serving: Calories 393 (Calories from Fat 51); Fat 6g (Saturated 1g); Cholesterol 55mg; Sodium 57mg; Carbohydrate 64g (Dietary Fiber 3g); Protein 22g

MAKE IT A MEAL

Butternut, buttercup or acorn squash sprinkled with cinnamon and drizzled with honey would be a great accompaniment to this fall-inspired dish.

Stacked Pork Enchiladas with Salsa Verde

5 SERVINGS PREP TIME: **20 MINUTES** START TO FINISH: **37 MINUTES**

¾ pound pork tenderloin

1 jar (16 ounces) green salsa (salsa verde)
(2 cups)

1 container (8 ounces) reduced-fat sour cream

1 large onion, chopped (1 cup)

1 medium yellow or green bell pepper,
chopped (1 cup)

3 cloves garlic, finely chopped

¾ cup shredded part-skim mozzarella cheese
(3 ounces)

4 fat-free flour tortillas (6 to 8 inches in
diameter)

*Betty's Tip*_____

Green salsa is often made with tomatillos,
which sometimes are called green tomatoes.
In truth, they're not tomatoes at all but a
completely different fruit, the tomatillo.

1. Heat oven to 400°. Spray square baking dish,
9 × 9 × 2 inches, with cooking spray.
Remove fat from pork. Cut pork into ¾-inch
cubes.

2. Mix salsa and sour cream and set aside. Spray
10-inch nonstick skillet with cooking spray
and heat over medium-high heat. Cook pork,
onion, bell pepper and garlic in skillet about
6 minutes, stirring occasionally, until pork is
no longer pink.

3. Stir 2 cups of the salsa mixture into pork
mixture. Cook uncovered over medium heat
1 minute, stirring frequently. Remove from
heat. Stir in ½ cup of the cheese.

4. Place 1 tortilla in baking dish. Top with one-
third of the pork mixture. Repeat layers
twice more. Top with remaining tortilla.
Spoon remaining salsa mixture on top.
Sprinkle with remaining ¼ cup cheese.
Cover loosely with aluminum foil and bake
about 10 minutes or until heated through.

1 serving: Calories 335 (Calories from Fat 80); Fat 9g
(Saturated 5g); Cholesterol 65mg; Sodium 440mg;
Carbohydrate 41g (Dietary Fiber 4g); Protein 27g

Stir-Fried Pork

4 SERVINGS PREP TIME: 5 MINUTES START TO FINISH: 20 MINUTES

1 pound pork tenderloin

2 cans (8 ounces each) pineapple chunks in juice, drained and juice reserved

3 tablespoons white vinegar

3 tablespoons mirin (rice wine) or sweet white wine or water

3 tablespoons reduced-sodium soy sauce

2 teaspoons cornstarch

1 teaspoon sesame or vegetable oil

1 small onion, chopped (¼ cup)

1 medium green bell pepper, cut into 1-inch pieces

1. Remove fat from pork. Cut pork into 1-inch cubes. Mix reserved pineapple juice, the vinegar, mirin, soy sauce and cornstarch.

2. Spray 12-inch nonstick skillet with cooking spray and heat over medium-high heat. Add oil and pork. Stir-fry 6 to 8 minutes or until no longer pink. Remove pork from skillet.

3. Spray skillet with cooking spray. Add onion and bell pepper. Stir-fry about 5 minutes or until onion is tender. Stir in pork, pineapple and juice mixture. Heat to boiling. Boil about 45 seconds, stirring constantly, until thickened.

1 serving: Calories 220 (Calories from Fat 45); Fat 5g (Saturated 2g); Cholesterol 65mg; Sodium 450mg; Carbohydrate 20g (Dietary Fiber 1g); Protein 25g

*Betty's Tip*_____

Mirin, also called rice wine, is a low-alcohol, sweet rice wine used in Japanese cooking.
_____

MAKE IT A MEAL

Serve the stir-fry over hot cooked rice.

Stir-Fried Pork with Mushrooms and Broccoli

4 SERVINGS PREP TIME: **15 MINUTES** START TO FINISH: **26 MINUTES**

2 cups uncooked instant brown rice

2¾ cups water

1 tablespoon cornstarch

¼ cup teriyaki marinade

½ teaspoon ground ginger

3 teaspoons canola oil

¾ pound pork boneless loin, trimmed of fat, cut into thin 2-inch strips

2 cups broccoli florets

1 small onion, cut into thin wedges

1 package (8 ounces) sliced mushrooms (3 cups)

1 medium red, yellow or orange bell pepper, cut into 1-inch pieces

2 cloves garlic, finely chopped

Hot cooked rice

1. Cook rice in 2¼ cups of the water as directed on package, omitting butter and salt.

2. Meanwhile, place cornstarch in small bowl or cup. Gradually stir in teriyaki marinade, ginger and remaining ½ cup water.

3. Heat 2 teaspoons of the oil in 12-inch non-stick skillet or wok over medium-high heat. Add pork and stir-fry 4 to 5 minutes or until no longer pink. Remove pork from skillet and keep warm.

4. Add remaining 1 teaspoon oil to skillet. Add broccoli, onion, mushrooms, bell pepper and garlic. Stir-fry 4 to 5 minutes or until vegetables are crisp-tender.

5. Stir cornstarch mixture into broccoli mixture. Add pork. Cook and stir until sauce is thickened. Serve over rice.

1 serving: Calories 410 (Calories from Fat 80); Fat 9g (Saturated 1.5g); Cholesterol 55mg; Sodium 770mg; Carbohydrate 56g (Dietary Fiber 5g); Protein 28g

SPEED SUPPER

A flavorful stir-fry usually requires a bit of chopping. Get all the ingredients chopped before starting to stir-fry; then it comes together very quickly. Customize this recipe by using any vegetables you like—even ones that are already cut up.

Skillet Pork Stew

4 SERVINGS PREP TIME: 5 MINUTES START TO FINISH: 30 MINUTES

1 pound pork boneless loin, cut into ½-inch pieces

1 jar (12 ounces) pork gravy

2 tablespoons ketchup

8 unpeeled small red potatoes, cut into fourths

1 cup fresh or frozen cut green beans

1. Spray 12-inch nonstick skillet with cooking spray and heat over medium-high heat. Cook pork in skillet 3 to 5 minutes, stirring frequently, until light brown.

2. Stir in gravy, ketchup and potatoes. Heat to boiling, then reduce heat to medium-low. Cover and cook 10 minutes.

3. Stir in beans. Cover and cook 5 to 10 minutes, stirring occasionally, until vegetables are tender.

1 serving: Calories 380 (Calories from Fat 80); Fat 9g (Saturated 4g); Cholesterol 55mg; Sodium 610mg; Carbohydrate 54g (Dietary Fiber 5g); Protein 26g

MAKE IT A MEAL

Serve this easy stew with bread, corn bread or biscuits.

Zesty Autumn Pork Stew

4 SERVINGS PREP TIME: **10 MINUTES** START TO FINISH: **30 MINUTES**

1 pound pork tenderloin

2 cloves garlic, finely chopped

2 medium sweet potatoes, peeled and cubed (2 cups)

1 cup coarsely chopped cabbage

1 medium green bell pepper, chopped (1 cup)

1 can (14½ ounces) fat-free chicken broth

1 teaspoon Cajun seasoning

1. Remove fat from pork. Cut pork into 1-inch cubes. Spray 4-quart Dutch oven with cooking spray and heat over medium-high heat. Cook pork in Dutch oven, stirring occasionally, until brown.

2. Stir in remaining ingredients. Heat to boiling; reduce heat. Cover and simmer about 15 minutes, stirring once, until sweet potatoes are tender.

1 serving: Calories 240 (Calories from Fat 45); Fat 5g (Saturated 2g); Cholesterol 70mg; Sodium 530mg; Carbohydrate 22g (Dietary Fiber 3g); Protein 30g

MAKE IT A MEAL

For a comfort meal, serve the stew with buttered noodles.

Slow-Cooker Hearty Pork Stew

6 SERVINGS PREP TIME: **25 MINUTES** START TO FINISH: **7 HOURS 10 MINUTES**

1½ pounds boneless pork loin roast, trimmed of fat, cut into 1-inch cubes

3 medium carrots, cut into ¼-inch slices (1½ cups)

1 medium onion, chopped (½ cup)

2 cups ½-inch cubes peeled parsnips

1½ cups 1-inch cubes peeled butternut squash

4 cups chicken broth

1 tablespoon chopped fresh or 1 teaspoon dried sage leaves

2 teaspoons chopped fresh or ¾ teaspoon dried thyme leaves

½ teaspoon pepper

2 tablespoons all-purpose flour

2 tablespoons butter or margarine, softened

1. Mix all ingredients except flour and butter in 4- to 5-quart slow cooker.

2. Cover and cook on low heat setting 6 to 7 hours.

3. In small bowl, mix flour and butter. Gradually stir into stew until blended. Increase heat setting to high. Cover and cook 30 to 45 minutes, stirring occasionally, until thickened.

1 serving: Calories 320 (Calories from Fat 130); Fat 14g (Saturated 6g); Cholesterol 85mg; Sodium 780mg; Carbohydrate 18g (Dietary Fiber 3g); Protein 30g

Betty's Tip

This recipe also works well with other root vegetables, such as sliced rutabagas or beets.

Grilled Honey-Mustard Pork Chops

4 SERVINGS PREP TIME: **5 MINUTES** START TO FINISH: **21 MINUTES**

4 pork boneless butterflied loin chops,
1 inch thick (about 1 pound)

¼ cup honey

2 tablespoons Dijon mustard

1 tablespoon orange juice

1 teaspoon cider vinegar

½ teaspoon Worcestershire sauce

Dash of onion powder

1. Heat coals or gas grill. Remove fat from pork. Mix remaining ingredients in small bowl.

2. Place pork on grill. Cover and grill pork 4 to 6 inches from medium heat 14 to 16 minutes, brushing occasionally with honey mixture and turning once, until slightly pink in center. Discard any remaining honey mixture.

1 serving: Calories 235 (Calories from Fat 70); Fat 8g (Saturated 3g); Cholesterol 65mg; Sodium 145mg; Carbohydrate 19g (Dietary Fiber 0g); Protein 22g

MAKE IT A MEAL

Serve these chops with boiled new potatoes and a salad of cubed jicama and watermelon tossed with lime juice and a teaspoon of sugar.

Tangy Barbecued Pork

6 SERVINGS PREP TIME: **10 MINUTES** START TO FINISH: **30 MINUTES**

3 pork boneless butterflied loin chops, ½ inch thick (about ¾ pound)

2 medium onions, cut lengthwise in half, then cut crosswise into thin slices

½ cup apricot spreadable fruit

½ cup fat-free sweet-spicy French dressing

3 tablespoons reduced-sodium onion soup mix (from 1½-ounce packet)

1 teaspoon red pepper sauce

Hot cooked brown rice, if desired

1. Remove fat from pork. Spray 12-inch nonstick skillet with cooking spray and heat over medium heat. Cook pork in skillet about 5 minutes, turning once, until brown. Remove from skillet.

2. Cook onions in same skillet over medium heat about 5 minutes, stirring frequently, until tender. Stir in spreadable fruit, dressing, soup mix (dry) and pepper sauce. Heat to boiling; reduce heat. Simmer uncovered 5 minutes, stirring occasionally.

3. Place pork on sauce. Spoon sauce over pork to cover. Cover and simmer about 5 minutes or until pork is slightly pink in center. Serve over rice if desired.

1 serving: Calories 185 (Calories from Fat 35); Fat 4g (Saturated 1g); Cholesterol 30mg; Sodium 530mg; Carbohydrate 28g (Dietary Fiber 2g); Protein 11g

MAKE IT A MEAL

All you need to complete this meal is coleslaw for a salad and your favorite bread or dinner rolls.

Greek Honey and Lemon Pork Chops

4 SERVINGS PREP TIME: **7 MINUTES** START TO FINISH: **15 MINUTES**

4 pork loin chops or ribs, ½ inch thick (about 1 pound)

1 tablespoon all-purpose Greek seasoning

1 teaspoon grated lemon peel

2 tablespoons lemon juice

3 tablespoons honey

1. Set oven control to broil. Place pork on rack in broiler pan.

2. Mix remaining ingredients. Brush honey mixture evenly on tops of pork chops.

3. Broil with tops 4 to 6 inches from heat 7 to 8 minutes, turning once and brushing with honey mixture, until slightly pink when cut near bone. Discard any remaining honey mixture.

1 serving: Calories 220 (Calories from Fat 61); Fat 7g (Saturated 2g); Cholesterol 62mg; Sodium 52mg; Carbohydrate 14g (Dietary Fiber 0g); Protein 25g

Betty's Tips

Add chopped fresh oregano to the honey mixture for authentic Greek flavor.

Greek seasoning, located in the spice aisle of your supermarket, includes salt, pepper, garlic, MSG, oregano, parsley and beef flavor.

MAKE IT A MEAL

Prepare a salad using fresh spinach, artichoke hearts, tomatoes and ripe olives for a Mediterranean-inspired meal.

Parmesan-Breaded Pork Chops

4 SERVINGS PREP TIME: **10 MINUTES** START TO FINISH: **30 MINUTES**

4 pork boneless butterflied loin chops, about ½ inch thick (about 1 pound)

⅓ cup Italian-style dry bread crumbs

2 tablespoons grated Parmesan cheese

¼ cup fat-free cholesterol-free egg product or 2 egg whites

1 can (14½ ounces) chunky tomatoes with olive oil, garlic and spices, undrained

1 can (8 ounces) tomato sauce

1 small green bell pepper, chopped (½ cup)

1. Remove fat from pork. Mix bread crumbs and cheese. Dip pork into egg product, then coat with crumb mixture. Spray 12-inch nonstick skillet with cooking spray and heat over medium heat. Cook pork in skillet about 5 minutes, turning once, until brown.

2. Stir in remaining ingredients. Heat to boiling; reduce heat. Cover and simmer 10 to 12 minutes, stirring occasionally, until pork is slightly pink in center.

1 serving: Calories 300 (Calories from Fat 125); Fat 14g (Saturated 5g); Cholesterol 65mg; Sodium 810mg; Carbohydrate 19g (Dietary Fiber 2g); Protein 27g

Betty's Tip

Italian-style bread crumbs are seasoned with a variety of herbs and spices. If you can't find the Italian-style, you can substitute seasoned bread crumbs (also available at grocery stores).

Plum-Mustard Pork Chops

4 SERVINGS PREP TIME: **5 MINUTES** START TO FINISH: **11 MINUTES**

4 boneless pork loin chops, ½ inch thick
(5 ounces each)

¼ teaspoon salt

¼ teaspoon pepper

¼ cup duck (plum) sauce or apricot jam

4 teaspoons yellow mustard

1. Heat 10-inch nonstick skillet over medium-high heat. Sprinkle pork chops with salt and pepper. Cook pork in skillet 5 to 6 minutes, turning after 3 minutes, until no longer pink in center.

2. Meanwhile, mix plum sauce and mustard in small bowl. Serve with pork.

1 serving: Calories 210 (Calories from Fat 70); Fat 8g (Saturated 3g); Cholesterol 65mg; Sodium 400mg; Carbohydrate 11g (Dietary Fiber 0g); Protein 23g

MAKE IT A MEAL
Serve with steamed snow (Chinese) pea pods.

Skillet Barbecue Pork Chops

4 SERVINGS PREP TIME: **5 MINUTES** START TO FINISH: **25 MINUTES**

4 pork loin or rib chops, ½ inch thick (about 1¼ pounds)

¼ teaspoon salt

⅛ teaspoon pepper

1 can (15 ounces) chunky tomato sauce with onions, celery and green bell peppers

2 tablespoons packed brown sugar

2 tablespoons apple cider vinegar

2 tablespoons Worcestershire sauce

1 teaspoon ground mustard

1. Spray 12-inch nonstick skillet with cooking spray and heat over medium heat. Sprinkle both sides of pork with salt and pepper. Cook pork in skillet about 5 minutes, turning once, until brown.

2. Mix remaining ingredients and add to skillet. Heat to boiling; reduce heat. Cover and simmer 10 to 15 minutes, stirring occasionally, until pork is slightly pink in center.

1 serving: Calories 230 (Calories from Fat 70); Fat 8g (Saturated 3g); Cholesterol 65mg; Sodium 900mg; Carbohydrate 16g (Dietary Fiber 1g); Protein 24g

MAKE IT A MEAL

Pierce 4 medium sweet potatoes of similar size to allow steam to escape. Arrange potatoes in circle on microwavable paper towel in microwave oven. Microwave uncovered on High 8 to 10 minutes or until tender. Let stand uncovered 5 minutes. Season with butter, salt and a dash of cinnamon, if desired.

Canadian Bacon and Spinach Sandwiches

4 SERVINGS PREP TIME: **5 MINUTES** START TO FINISH: **12 MINUTES**

4 slices French bread, 1 inch thick

1 cup bite-size pieces washed fresh spinach leaves

2 tablespoons ranch dressing

4 slices (2 ounces each) Canadian-style bacon

4 slices (1 ounce each) Swiss cheese

1. Set oven control to broil. Place bread on rack in broiler pan or cookie sheet. Broil with tops 4 to 6 inches from heat, 1 to 2 minutes on each side or until toasted.

2. Mix spinach and dressing. Spoon spinach onto toasted bread. Broil about 2 minutes or until hot. Top with bacon and cheese. Broil about 1 minute or until cheese is melted.

1 sandwich: Calories 280 (Calories from Fat 135); Fat 15g (Saturated 7g); Cholesterol 55mg; Sodium 1,010mg; Carbohydrate 15g (Dietary Fiber 1g); Protein 22g

SPEED SUPPER

Fresh spinach is usually available pre-washed and packaged in the produce section of large supermarkets—and it helps make it a snap to whip up these sandwiches.

MAKE IT A MEAL

Serve wedges of Gala or Golden Delicious apples on the side for a no-cook accompaniment.

Sausage Skillet Supper

6 SERVINGS PREP TIME: **10 MINUTES** START TO FINISH: **35 MINUTES**

3 tablespoons vegetable oil

1 bag (24 ounces) frozen diced potatoes with onions and peppers

½ teaspoon dried oregano or basil leaves

½ teaspoon pepper

2 cups broccoli flowerets

1 ring (about ¾ pound) bologna or fully cooked smoked sausage

3 slices process American cheese, cut diagonally in half

1. Heat oil in 10-inch skillet over medium-high heat. Add potatoes, oregano and pepper. Cover and cook 8 to 10 minutes, stirring occasionally, until potatoes are light brown.

2. Stir in broccoli, then add bologna. Cover and cook about 15 minutes or until bologna is hot. Top with cheese. Cover and heat until cheese is melted.

1 serving: Calories 500 (Calories from Fat 270); Fat 30g (Saturated 11g); Cholesterol 45mg; Sodium 1,750mg; Carbohydrate 47g (Dietary Fiber 4g); Protein 15g

Ham with Cabbage and Apples

4 SERVINGS PREP TIME: **10 MINUTES** START TO FINISH: **25 MINUTES**

4 cups coleslaw mix or shredded cabbage

1 tablespoon packed brown sugar

1 tablespoon cider vinegar

⅛ teaspoon pepper

1 large onion, chopped (1 cup)

1 large green cooking apple, sliced

1 fully cooked ham slice, about ½ inch thick (1 pound)

1. Spray 10-inch nonstick skillet with cooking spray and heat over medium heat. Cook all ingredients except ham in skillet about 5 minutes, stirring frequently, until apple is crisp-tender.

2. Place ham on cabbage mixture and reduce heat. Cover and cook about 10 minutes or until ham is hot.

1 serving: Calories 215 (Calories from Fat 70); Fat 8g (Saturated 3g); Cholesterol 50mg; Sodium 1,240mg; Carbohydrate 19g (Dietary Fiber 3g); Protein 20g

MAKE IT A MEAL
Horseradish Mashed Potatoes

4 SERVINGS PREP TIME: **5 MINUTES** START TO FINISH: **25 MINUTES**

4 medium unpeeled boiling potatoes (about 1½ pounds), cut into ½-inch slices

⅓ cup plain low-fat or fat-free yogurt

1 tablespoon prepared horseradish

½ teaspoon salt

2 to 4 tablespoons fat-free (skim) milk

Chopped fresh parsley, if desired

1. Heat 1 inch water to boiling in 3-quart saucepan. Add potatoes and heat to boiling. Reduce heat to low and cook about 15 minutes or until tender; drain. Return potatoes to saucepan. Shake pan with potatoes over low heat to dry, then remove from heat.

2. Mash potatoes until no lumps remain. Beat in yogurt, horseradish and salt. Add milk in small amounts, beating after each addition (amount of milk needed to make potatoes smooth and fluffy depends on the kind of potatoes used). Beat vigorously until potatoes are light and fluffy. Sprinkle with parsley if desired.

1 serving: Calories 130 (Calories from Fat 0); Fat 0g (Saturated 0g); Cholesterol 1mg; Sodium 180mg; Carbohydrate 31g (Dietary Fiber 3g); Protein 4g

Betty's Tip

If you prefer a milder flavor, use horseradish sauce in place of the prepared horseradish and decrease the yogurt to ¼ cup. Horseradish sauce is higher in calories and fat than prepared horseradish. You can find it next to the mayonnaise in your supermarket.

Ham with Spiced Peaches

6 SERVINGS PREP TIME: **10 MINUTES** START TO FINISH: **45 MINUTES**

6 slices fully cooked lower-fat lower-sodium ham, ¼ inch thick (about 1 pound)

6 medium sweet potatoes or yams (2 pounds), peeled and cut into 1½-inch slices

½ cup water

1 jar (10 ounces) apricot or orange marmalade spreadable fruit

¼ cup packed brown sugar

½ teaspoon ground cinnamon

⅛ teaspoon ground red pepper (cayenne)

1 bag (1 pound) frozen sliced peaches, partially thawed and drained

1. Heat oven to 375°. Arrange ham in ungreased rectangular baking dish, 13 × 9 × 2 inches.

2. Heat sweet potatoes and water to boiling in 3-quart saucepan; reduce heat. Cover and simmer about 10 minutes or until potatoes are almost tender; drain.

3. Meanwhile, heat spreadable fruit, brown sugar, cinnamon and red pepper in 1-quart saucepan over medium heat about 5 minutes, stirring constantly, until hot and bubbly.

4. Arrange sweet potatoes and peaches on ham. Pour sauce over top. Cover and bake 15 minutes. Bake uncovered about 5 to 10 minutes longer until heated through.

1 serving: Calories 370 (Calories from Fat 25); Fat 3g (Saturated 1g); Cholesterol 35mg; Sodium 580mg; Carbohydrate 85g (Dietary Fiber 8g); Protein 15g

MAKE IT A MEAL
Sweet-Sour Coleslaw

6 SERVINGS PREP TIME: **5 MINUTES** START TO FINISH: **15 MINUTES**

1 egg

¼ cup sugar

¼ cup white vinegar

2 tablespoons water

2 tablespoons margarine or butter

1 teaspoon salt

½ teaspoon ground mustard

1 pound green cabbage, finely shredded or chopped

1 small bell pepper, chopped

1. Beat egg until thick and lemon colored.

2. Heat sugar, vinegar, water, margarine, salt and mustard to boiling in small saucepan, stirring constantly. Gradually stir half of it into the egg, then stir back into saucepan.

3. Cook over low heat, stirring constantly, until thickened, about 5 minutes. Place cabbage and bell pepper in large serving bowl. Pour sauce over cabbage and bell pepper; toss.

1 serving: Calories 80 (Calories from Fat 35); Fat 4g (Saturated 1g); Cholesterol 2mg; Sodium 350mg; Carbohydrate 10g (Dietary Fiber 1g); Protein 2g

Picante Pork Chili

4 SERVINGS PREP TIME: **6 MINUTES** START TO FINISH: **21 MINUTES**

1 medium onion, chopped (½ cup)

1 medium green bell pepper, chopped (1 cup)

1 clove garlic, finely chopped

½ pound ground pork

1 cup salsa

1 teaspoon chili powder

1 can (15 to 16 ounces) pinto beans, rinsed and drained

1 can (16 ounces) whole tomatoes, undrained

1. Cook onion, bell pepper, garlic and pork in 3-quart saucepan over medium heat, stirring frequently, until pork is no longer pink; drain if necessary.

2. Stir in remaining ingredients, breaking up tomatoes. Heat to boiling; reduce heat. Cover and simmer 10 minutes.

1 serving: Calories 280 (Calories from Fat 90); Fat 10g (Saturated 3g); Cholesterol 35mg; Sodium 850mg; Carbohydrate 37g (Dietary Fiber 10g); Protein 20g

MAKE IT A MEAL

Serve guacamole with baked tortilla chips on the side.

Curry Pork Sausage Couscous

4 SERVINGS PREP TIME: **5 MINUTES** START TO FINISH: **20 MINUTES**

1½ cups uncooked couscous

½ pound bulk pork sausage

1 large onion, chopped (1 cup)

½ cup pistachio nuts, coarsely chopped

1 teaspoon curry powder

1 teaspoon salt

2 cloves garlic, finely chopped

2 tablespoons chopped fresh parsley

*Betty's Tip*_____

Ground pork or mild bulk Italian sausage also could be used in this dish.

1. Prepare couscous as directed on package.

2. While couscous is standing, cook sausage, onion, nuts, curry powder, salt and garlic in 10-inch skillet over medium heat, stirring occasionally, until sausage is no longer pink; drain.

3. Stir in couscous and parsley. Cook over medium heat about 5 minutes, stirring occasionally, until mixture is hot.

1 serving: Calories 483 (Calories from Fat 164); Fat 18g (Saturated 4g); Cholesterol 41mg; Sodium 879mg; Carbohydrate 59g (Dietary Fiber 6g); Protein 21g

MAKE IT A MEAL

Serve with cooked broccoli. To prepare, trim off large leaves from 1½ pounds broccoli and remove tough ends of lower stems. Wash and peel stalk if desired. Cut lengthwise into ½-inch-wide spears. Heat 1 inch water (salted, if desired) to boiling. Add spears. Cover and heat to boiling; reduce heat. Boil 10 to 12 minutes or until crisp-tender. Season to taste with salt, pepper, butter or lemon juice, if desired.

Italian Sausage Pot Pies

4 SERVINGS PREP TIME: **15 MINUTES** START TO FINISH: **45 MINUTES**

1 pound bulk Italian sausage or ground beef

1 medium onion, chopped (½ cup)

1 small green bell pepper, chopped (½ cup)

½ cup sliced mushrooms

1 can (8 ounces) pizza sauce

1 cup shredded mozzarella cheese (4 ounces)

1 cup Original Bisquick®

¼ cup boiling water

Betty's Tips

For a special holiday treat, use a small cookie cutter to cut a festive shape out of the dough circle before putting it on the sausage mixture. For itty-bitty pastry treats, place the cut-outs on a cookie sheet and bake in a 375° oven for about 15 minutes or until light golden brown.

1. Heat oven to 375°. Grease four 10- to 12-ounce casseroles.

2. Cook sausage, onion and bell pepper in 10-inch skillet over medium heat, stirring frequently, until sausage is no longer pink; drain. Stir in mushrooms and pizza sauce. Heat to boiling; reduce heat. Simmer uncovered 5 minutes, stirring occasionally. Spoon sausage mixture into casseroles. Sprinkle ¼ cup of the cheese over each.

3. Stir Bisquick and boiling water. Beat vigorously 20 strokes. Place dough on surface sprinkled with Bisquick and gently roll to coat. Shape into ball and knead about 10 times or until smooth.

4. Divide dough into 4 balls. Pat each ball into circle the size of the diameter of the casseroles. Make cut in each circle with knife to vent steam. Place circles on sausage mixture in casseroles. Bake 15 to 20 minutes or until light golden brown.

1 serving: Calories 520 (Calories from Fat 295); Fat 33g (Saturated 12g); Cholesterol 80mg; Sodium 1,540mg; Carbohydrate 29g (Dietary Fiber 2g); Protein 28g

INDEX

Underscored page references indicate sidebar notes. **Boldfaced** page references indicate photographs.

Mangoes
    Fresh Melon Salad, 158, **159**
    Tropical Chicken Salad, 167
Meat. *See* Beef; Pork
Meatballs, preparing, from meat loaf recipe, <u>228</u>
Meat loaves
    Mini Greek Meat Loaves with Tzatziki Sauce, 229
    Mini Meat Loaves, 228
Melon
    Crunchy Jicama and Melon Salad, 91
    Fresh Melon Salad, 158, **159**
Millet
    Beef and Millet Stew in Bread Bowls, **214**, 215
Monterey Jack cheese
    Cheese Enchiladas, 48
    Cheesy Double-Bean Chili, 89
    Chicken Quesadilla Sandwiches, 55
    Mixed-Bean Stew with Cottage Dumplings, 92
    Spanish Rice Bake, **30**, 31
    Vegetable Tortillas, 75
Mozzarella cheese
    Canadian Bacon Whole Wheat Pizza, **24**, 25
    Indian Curried Turkey Pizzas, 22
    Italian Sausage Pot Pies, 260, **261**
    Mozzarella and Tomato Melts, 53
    Quick Italian Chicken Sandwich, 165
    Skillet Chicken Parmigiana, 142
    Vegetable-Cheese Bake, 50
Mushrooms
    Beef Cubed Steaks with Mushroom-Cream Sauce, 218
    Beef Stroganoff Casserole, **198**, 199
    Bok Choy and Cashew Stir-Fry, 67
    Flounder with Mushrooms and Wine, 106
    Halibut and Asparagus Stir-Fry, 127
    Italian Barley and Bean Pilaf, 80
    Italian Frittata with Vinaigrette Tomatoes, **36**, 37
    Lentil Stew, 96
    Mushroom-Pepper Whole Wheat Sandwiches, **72**, 73
    Pan-Roasted Garden Vegetables with Eggs, 46
    Portabella Stroganoff, 15
    Ravioli with Tomato-Alfredo Sauce, 13
    Salmon-Pasta Toss, **116**, 117
    Stir-Fried Pork with Mushrooms and Broccoli, 241
    Stuffed Pasta Shells, **2**, 3
    Sweet-and-Sour Oriental Pasta Salad, 78
    Tilapia Florentine, 120
    wild, note about, <u>155</u>
    Wild Mushroom Herbed Chicken, 155

Mustard
    Creole, note about, <u>125</u>
    Creole Mustard–Broiled Whitefish, 125

N

Nuts
    Bok Choy and Cashew Stir-Fry, 67
    cashews, storing, <u>78</u>
    Fruity Chicken Salad with Spring Greens and Pecans, 166
    Nut-Crusted Pork Medallions, 235
    Peas and Almonds, 196, **197**
    Sole with Almonds, 118
    Sweet-and-Sour Oriental Pasta Salad, 78
    toasting, <u>98</u>
    Vegetable Kung Pao, 66

O

Olives
    Quick Chicken with Olives and Tomatoes, 162
One-dish meals
    Baked Ziti and Bean Casserole, 14
    Beef and Kasha Mexicana, 224, **225**
    Beef and Millet Stew in Bread Bowls, **214**, 215
    Cheesy Chicken Casserole, 177
    Chicken and Pasta Stir-Fry, 6
    Chicken Pasta Primavera, 7
    Creamy Bow-Ties with Ham and Vegetables, 12
    Creamy Chicken and Corn with Fettuccine, 176
    Italian Turkey-Couscous Salad, 28
    Lemon and Herb Salmon Packets, 114
    Lemon-Dill Salmon and Potatoes, 112
    Mediterranean Shrimp with Bulgur, **132**, 133
    Noodles and Peanut Sauce Salad Bowl, **16**, 17
    Pork Lo Mein, **10**, 11
    Quick Paella, 134
    Salmon-Pasta Toss, **116**, 117
    Sausage Skillet Supper, 254
    Shanghai Chicken and Noodles, 8
    Slow-Cooker Chicken-Barley Stew, 168
    Stir-Fried Pork with Mushrooms and Broccoli, 241
    Szechuan Chicken and Pasta, 9
    Tuscan Rigatoni with White Beans, 4
    Vegetable Stew with Polenta, 26

Conversion Chart

These equivalents have been slightly rounded to make measuring easier.

VOLUME MEASUREMENTS

U.S.	Imperial	Metric
¼ tsp	–	1 ml
½ tsp	–	2 ml
1 tsp	–	5 ml
1 Tbsp	–	15 ml
2 Tbsp (1 oz)	1 fl oz	30 ml
¼ cup (2 oz)	2 fl oz	60 ml
⅓ cup (3 oz)	3 fl oz	80 ml
½ cup (4 oz)	4 fl oz	120 ml
⅔ cup (5 oz)	5 fl oz	160 ml
¾ cup (6 oz)	6 fl oz	180 ml
1 cup (8 oz)	8 fl oz	240 ml

WEIGHT MEASUREMENTS

U.S.	Metric
1 oz	30 g
2 oz	60 g
4 oz (¼ lb)	115 g
5 oz (⅓ lb)	145 g
6 oz	170 g
7 oz	200 g
8 oz (½ lb)	230 g
10 oz	285 g
12 oz (¾ lb)	340 g
14 oz	400 g
16 oz (1 lb)	455 g
2.2 lb	1 kg

LENGTH MEASUREMENTS

U.S.	Metric
¼"	0.6 cm
½"	1.25 cm
1"	2.5 cm
2"	5 cm
4"	11 cm
6"	15 cm
8"	20 cm
10"	25 cm
12" (1')	30 cm

PAN SIZES

U.S.	Metric
8" cake pan	20 × 4 cm sandwich or cake tin
9" cake pan	23 × 3.5 cm sandwich or cake tin
11" × 7" baking pan	28 × 18 cm baking tin
13" × 9" baking pan	32.5 × 23 cm baking tin
15" × 10" baking pan	38 × 25.5 cm baking tin (Swiss roll tin)
1½ qt baking dish	1.5 liter baking dish
2 qt baking dish	2 liter baking dish
2 qt rectangular baking dish	30 × 19 cm baking dish
9" pie plate	22 × 4 or 23 × 4 cm pie plate
7" or 8" springform pan	18 or 20 cm springform or loose-bottom cake tin
9" × 5" loaf pan	23 × 13 cm or 2 lb narrow loaf tin or pâté tin

TEMPERATURES

Fahrenheit	Centigrade	Gas
140°	60°	–
160°	70°	–
180°	80°	–
225°	105°	¼
250°	120°	½
275°	135°	1
300°	150°	2
325°	160°	3
350°	180°	4
375°	190°	5
400°	200°	6
425°	220°	7
450°	230°	8
475°	245°	9
500°	260°	–